AFGHANS

FOR ALL SEASONS

Here at last — in a single, handy volume — is a spectacular collection of favorite crocheted afghans from Leisure Arts. Compiled with the four seasons in mind, it offers 52 afghans in all — one for every week if you want to keep your fingers flying!

As you turn the pages, you'll find yourself taking a beautiful walk through the seasons. Blooming with soft charm and pretty colors, the spring afghans are delightfully delicate. The summer spreads will remind you of sunny days meant for picnics and star-spangled celebrations. The autumn throws capture the splendid hues of the harvest season, and many of the winter wraps are crocheted in rich, warm tones.

Afghans for All Seasons has a variety of patterns that both beginning and advanced crocheters will find easy to follow. There are afghans to make for everyone in the family, from masculine designs for dad and feminine frills for mom to bright throws for children and cuddly cover-ups for baby.

For more than 20 years, stitchers have turned to Leisure Arts to find top-quality designs and first-rate instructions for crochet and other needlecrafts. Here now are the tried and true favorites from the Leisure Arts archives — all in one convenient collection! Enjoy Afghans for All Seasons, and happy crocheting!

LEISURE ARTS, INC.
and
OXMOOR HOUSE, INC.

D0471990

EDITORIAL STAFF

Editor-in-Chief: Anne Van Wagner Childs
Executive Director: Sandra Graham Case
Executive Editor: Susan Frantz Wiles
Publications Director: Carla Bentley
Creative Art Director: Gloria Bearden
Production Art Director: Melinda Stout

PRODUCTION

Managing Editor: Barbara B. Rondeau
Senior Editor: Cathy Hardy
Editorial Assistants: Jennine Korejko, Anita Lewis,
  Lee Tribett, Sherry Berry, Shobha Govindan,
  Linda Luder, Mary Jo Massery, Lois Phillips,
  Teri Sargent, and Cate Wallace
Production Assistant: Debra Nettles

EDITORIAL

Senior Editor: Linda L. Trimble
Senior Editorial Writer: Darla Burdette Kelsay
Editorial Writer: Laurie R. Burleson
Associate Editor: Dorothy Latimer Johnson

ART

Book/Magazine Art Director: Diane Ghegan
Senior Production Artist: Ashley Cole
Creative Art Assistant: Judith Howington Merritt
Photography Stylists: Christina Tiano, Karen Smart
  Hall, Jan Nobles, Lynn Bell, Rhonda Hestir, Pat
  Farmer, and Charlisa Erwin Parker
Typesetters: Cindy Lumpkin and Stephanie Cordero

BUSINESS STAFF

Publisher: Steve Patterson
Controller: Tom Siebenmorgen
Retail Sales Director: Richard Tignor
Retail Marketing Director: Pam Stebbins
Retail Customer Services Director: Margaret
  Sweetin
Marketing Manager: Russ Barnett
Executive Director of Marketing and Circulation:
  Guy A. Crossley
Fulfillment Manager: Byron L. Taylor
Print Production: Nancy Reddick Lister and
  Laura Lockhart

Afghans for All Seasons
from the *Crochet Treasury* series
Published by Leisure Arts, Inc., and Oxmoor House, Inc.

Library of Congress Catalog Number: 93-077419
Hardcover ISBN 0-942237-23-4
Softcover ISBN 0-942237-24-2

Table Of Contents

SPRING

With the gentle warming of the weather, dainty flowers
come springing up everywhere to greet the sunshine. Their
delicate beauty and sweet fragrance delight the senses, stirring
a feeling of wonder in our hearts. This collection of afghans
is blooming with the soft charm of springtime blossoms.
Lovely for cool spring days, the wraps are created with
classic patterns worked in pretty colors.

FLOWER PATCH AFGHAN

*Like lavender and lace, this decidedly feminine afghan
creates a gentle feeling. Handcrafted warmth and heather-toned
blossoms make it an irresistible comfort.*

Finished Size: Approximately 50" x 70"

MATERIALS
Worsted Weight Yarn, approximately:
Color A (Light Yellow) - 3½ ounces,
(100 grams, 220 yards)
Color B (Lavender) - 21 ounces,
(600 grams, 1,325 yards)
Color C (Green) - 17½ ounces,
(500 grams, 1,100 yards)
Color D (Ecru) - 21 ounces,
(600 grams, 1,325 yards)
Crochet hook, size I (5.50 mm) **or** size needed for
gauge
Yarn needle

GAUGE: Rnds 1-3 = 4½"
One Motif = 10"

MOTIF (Make 35)

With Color A ch 4, join with slip st to form a ring.
Rnd 1 (Right side): Ch 3, (YO, insert hook in ring, YO
and pull up a loop even with hook) twice, YO and
draw through all 5 loops on hook, ch 2, ★ (YO, insert
hook in ring, YO and pull up a loop even with hook) 3
times, YO and draw through all 7 loops on hook **(Puff
St made)**, ch 2; repeat from ★ 6 times **more**; join with
slip st to first Puff St, finish off: 8 Puff Sts.
Rnd 2: With **right** side facing, join Color B with slip st
in any Puff St; ch 1, sc in same st, (2 dc, ch 1, 2 dc) in
next ch-2 sp, ★ sc in next Puff St, (2 dc, ch 1, 2 dc) in
next ch-2 sp; repeat from ★ around; join with slip st to
first sc.
Rnd 3: Ch 1, sc in same st, (3 dc, ch 1, 3 dc) in next
ch-1 sp, ★ sc in next sc, (3 dc, ch 1, 3 dc) in next ch-1 sp;
repeat from ★ around; join with slip st to first sc.
Rnd 4: Slip st in first dc, ch 1, sc in same st, (4 dc, ch 1,
4 dc) in next ch-1 sp, skip next 2 dc, sc in next dc, ch 1,
★ skip next sc, sc in next dc, (4 dc, ch 1, 4 dc) in next
ch-1 sp, skip next 2 dc, sc in next dc, ch 1; repeat from ★
around; join with slip st to first sc: 8 Petals.
Rnd 5: Turn; slip st in first ch-1 sp, ch 1, turn; sc in
same sp, ch 6 **loosely**, ★ working **behind** Rnd 4, skip
next ch-1 sp, sc in next ch-1 sp (between Petals),
ch 6 **loosely**; repeat from ★ around; join with slip st to
first sc, finish off.

Rnd 6: With **right** side facing, join Color C with slip st
in first ch of any ch-6 loop; ch 3 **(counts as first dc, now
and throughout)**, working in each ch and in each sc
around, dc in next ch, 2 dc in next ch, ch 1 (corner),
2 dc in next ch, ★ dc in next 12 sts, 2 dc in next ch, ch 1,
2 dc in next ch; repeat from ★ 2 times **more**, dc in last
10 sts; join with slip st to first dc: 64 dc.
Rnd 7: Ch 3, dc in next 3 dc, (2 dc, ch 1, 2 dc) in next
ch-1 sp, ★ dc in each dc across to next corner ch-1 sp,
(2 dc, ch 1, 2 dc) in ch-1 sp; repeat from ★ 2 times **more**,
dc in each dc across; join with slip st to first dc,
finish off: 80 dc.
Rnd 8: With **right** side facing, join Color D with slip st
in any ch-1 sp; ch 1, 3 sc in same sp, ★ sc in each dc
across to next corner ch-1 sp, 3 sc in ch-1 sp; repeat
from ★ 2 times **more**, sc in each dc across; join with
slip st to first sc, finish off: 92 sc.
Note: Work V-st as follows: (Dc, ch 1, dc) in stitch or
space indicated.
Rnd 9: With **right** side facing, join Color B with slip st
in first sc of any 3-sc group; ch 4, dc in same st, work
V-st in next 2 sc, (skip next 2 sc, work V-st in next sc) 6
times, skip next 2 sc, ★ work V-st in next 3 sc, (skip
next 2 sc, work V-st in next sc) 6 times, skip next 2 sc;
repeat from ★ around; join with slip st to third ch of
beginning ch-4, finish off: 36 ch-1 sps.
Rnd 10: With **right** side facing, join Color C with slip st
in any corner V-st (ch-1 sp); ch 4, work V-st in same sp
and in next 8 V-sts, ★ dc in next V-st, ch 1, work V-st in
same sp and in next 8 V-sts; repeat from ★ around; join
with slip st to third ch of beginning ch-4, finish off:
40 ch-1 sps.
Rnd 11: With **right** side facing, skip first ch-1 sp and
join Color D with slip st in next ch-1 sp; ch 4, dc in
same sp, work V-st in next 9 ch-1 sps, ch 1, ★ work V-st
in next 10 ch-1 sps, ch 1; repeat from ★ around; join
with slip st to third ch of beginning ch-4: 44 ch-1 sps.
Rnd 12: Ch 1, sc in same st, ★ sc in each ch-1 sp and in
each dc across to next corner ch-1 sp, 3 sc in corner
ch-1 sp; repeat from ★ around; join with slip st to first
sc, finish off.

JOINING

Afghan is assembled by whipstitching 7 Motifs into 5 vertical strips, with **right** sides together and working through inside loops, and then by whipstitching strips **(Fig. 23b, page 141)**.

EDGING

With **right** side facing, join Color D with slip st in any sc; ch 1, sc evenly around, working 3 sc in each corner sc; join with slip st to first sc, finish off.

SPRING RIPPLE

Ripples of peach give this textured throw a splash of springtime color. Popcorn stitches add extra interest.

Finished Size: Approximately 42" x 59"

MATERIALS

Worsted Weight Yarn, approximately:
   Main Color (Mint) - 31 ounces,
      (880 grams, 2,040 yards)
   Contrasting Color (Peach) - 8 ounces,
      (230 grams, 525 yards)
Crochet hook, size I (5.50 mm) **or** size needed for gauge

GAUGE: In pattern, 48 sts (2 repeats) = 10½"
                    5 rows = 4"
      Gauge Swatch: (10½" x 4")
      Ch 53 **loosely**.
      Work same as Afghan for 5 rows: 51 sts.
      Finish off.

With MC, ch 197 **loosely**.

Row 1 (Right side): YO, insert hook in fourth ch from hook and pull up a loop, YO and draw through 2 loops on hook, (YO, insert hook in **next** ch and pull up a loop, YO and draw through 2 loops on hook) twice, YO and draw through all 4 loops on hook, dc in next 9 chs, 5 dc in next ch, dc in next 9 chs, ★ work decrease as follows: (YO, insert hook in **next** st and pull up a loop, YO and draw through 2 loops on hook) 5 times, YO and draw through all 6 loops on hook **(decrease made)**, dc in next 9 chs, 5 dc in next ch, dc in next 9 chs; repeat from ★ across to last 4 chs, work end decrease as follows: (YO, insert hook in **next** st and pull up a loop, YO and draw through 2 loops on hook) 3 times, YO and draw through all 4 loops on hook **(end decrease made)**, dc in last ch: 195 sts.

Note: Work in Back Loops Only throughout **(Fig. 18, page 140)**.

Row 2: Ch 3, turn; work beginning decrease as follows: (YO, insert hook in **next** st and pull up a loop, YO and draw through 2 loops on hook) 3 times, YO and draw through all 4 loops on hook **(beginning decrease made)**, dc in next 9 sts, 5 dc in next st, dc in next 9 sts, ★ decrease, dc in next 9 sts, 5 dc in next st, dc in next 9 sts; repeat from ★ across to last 4 sts, work end decrease, dc in top of beginning ch.

Row 3 (Eyelet row): Ch 3, turn; work beginning decrease, ch 1, (skip next st, dc in next st, ch 1) 4 times, skip next st, 5 dc in next st, ch 1, (skip next st, dc in next st, ch 1) 4 times, ★ skip next st, decrease, ch 1, (skip next st, dc in next st, ch 1) 4 times, skip next st, 5 dc in next st, ch 1, (skip next st, dc in next st, ch 1) 4 times; repeat from ★ across to last 5 sts, skip next st, work end decrease, dc in top of beginning ch.

Row 4: With CC **(Fig. 21, page 141)**, repeat Row 2.

Note: Work Popcorn as follows: 5 Dc in dc indicated, drop loop from hook, insert hook in first dc of 5-dc group, hook dropped loop and draw through **(Fig. 12, page 137)**, ch 1 to close.

Row 5: Ch 3, turn; work beginning decrease, (ch 1, skip next dc, work Popcorn in next dc) 5 times, ch 2, work Popcorn in same dc as last Popcorn, ch 1, (skip next dc, work Popcorn in next dc, ch 1) 4 times, ★ skip next dc, decrease, (ch 1, skip next dc, work Popcorn in next dc) 5 times, ch 2, work Popcorn in same dc as last Popcorn, ch 1, (skip next dc, work Popcorn in next dc, ch 1) 4 times; repeat from ★ across to last 5 sts, skip next dc, work end decrease, dc in top of beginning ch.

Row 6: Ch 3, turn; work beginning decrease, (dc in next ch, dc in closing ch of next Popcorn) 4 times, 7 dc

in next ch-2 sp, (dc in next Popcorn, dc in next ch) 4 times, ★ decrease, (dc in next ch, dc in next Popcorn) 4 times, 7 dc in next ch-2 sp, (dc in next Popcorn, dc in next ch) 4 times; repeat from ★ across to last 4 sts, work end decrease, dc in top of beginning ch.

Row 7: With MC, repeat Row 3.

Row 8: Repeat Row 2.

Rows 9 and 10: Repeat Rows 5 and 6.

Row 11: Repeat Row 3.

Rows 12-14: With CC, repeat Rows 4-6.

Row 15: With MC, repeat Row 3.
With MC, repeat Row 2 until afghan measures approximately 47″ from beginning ch, ending by working a **wrong** side row.
Repeat Rows 3-15.
With MC, repeat Row 2 twice.
Finish off.

Add fringe *(Figs. 25a & b, page 142)*.

VICTORIAN THROW

Reminiscent of an elegant era, our Victorian Throw features a lacy diamond pattern worked in filet crochet. We fashioned ours with cotton yarn, but you can use any worsted weight yarn.

Finished Size: Approximately 45″ x 65″

MATERIALS
100% Cotton Worsted Weight Yarn, approximately:
57 ounces, (1,610 grams, 2,875 yards)
Crochet hook, size G (4.00 mm) **or** size needed for gauge

GAUGE: 16 dc and 8 rows = 4″

Ch 264 **loosely.**

Row 1 (Right side): Dc in fourth ch from hook and in next 2 chs, † (ch 2, skip next 2 chs, dc in next ch) twice, ch 2, skip next 2 chs, dc in next 4 chs †, repeat from † to † once **more,** ★ (ch 2, skip next 2 chs, dc in next ch) twice, ch 2, skip next 2 chs, dc in next 34 chs, repeat from † to † 3 times; repeat from ★ 2 times **more.**

Row 2: [Ch 5, turn, dc in fourth ch from hook and in next ch, dc in next dc **(beginning increase made)**], [ch 2, skip 2 dc, dc in next dc **(Space over Block made)**], [ch 2, dc in next dc **(Space over Space made)**],

work Space, [2 dc in next ch-2 sp, dc in next dc **(Block over Space made)**], work Space, (work Block, work 3 Spaces) twice, ★ † [dc in next 3 dc **(Block over Block made)**] 9 times, (work 3 Spaces, work Block) twice, work Space †, (work Block, work 3 Spaces) twice; repeat from ★ once **more,** then repeat from † to † once, work Block, work 3 Spaces, work **end increase** as follows: [YO, insert hook into base of last dc and pull up a loop, YO and draw through one loop on hook, (YO and draw through 2 loops on hook) twice] 3 times.

Rows 3-6: Follow Chart.

Row 7: [Turn, slip st in first 4 dc, ch 3 **(beginning decrease made)**], follow Chart across, leaving last 3 sts unworked.

Rows 8-11: Follow Chart.

Rows 12-91: Repeat Rows 2-11, 8 times.
Finish off.

Optional: With **right** side facing, join yarn with slip st in first st; ch 1, sc evenly across; finish off.
Repeat for second end.

KEY
▨ - 1 Block = 3 dc
☐ - 1 Space = ch 2, dc

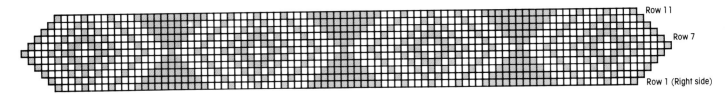

DIAMOND CLASSIC

With its generous clusters forming a pattern of diamonds,
this lacy afghan has rich texture and classic styling.

Finished Size: Approximately 46" x 63"

MATERIALS
Worsted Weight Yarn, approximately:
40 ounces, (1,140 grams, 2,630 yards)
Crochet hook, size I (5.50 mm) **or** size needed for
gauge

GAUGE: In pattern, sc, (Lace St, sc) 5 times
and 8 rows = 4"

PATTERN STITCHES
LACE STITCH
Ch 3, dc in third ch from hook.
CLUSTER (worked across 5 dc)
★ YO, insert hook in **next** dc, YO and pull up a loop,
YO and draw through 2 loops on hook; repeat from ★
4 times **more**, YO and draw through all 6 loops on hook
(Figs. 9c & d, page 135). Push Cluster to **right** side.

Ch 226 **loosely**.
Row 1 (Right side): Sc in second ch from hook,
(work Lace St, skip next 3 chs, sc in next ch) across:
56 Lace Sts.
Note: Loop a short piece of yarn around any stitch to
mark last row as **right** side.
Row 2: Ch 4 **(counts as first dc plus ch 1, now and
throughout)**, turn; sc in first Lace St (ch-3 sp), 5 dc in
Back Loop Only of next sc *(Fig. 18, page 140)*, sc in next
Lace St, ★ (work Lace St, sc in next Lace St) 5 times,
5 dc in Back Loop Only of next sc, sc in next Lace St;
repeat from ★ across to last sc, ch 1, dc in last sc:
10 5-dc groups.
Row 3: Ch 1, turn; sc in first dc, work Lace St, work
Cluster, work Lace St, ★ (sc in next Lace St, work
Lace St) 5 times, work Cluster, work Lace St; repeat
from ★ across to last dc, sc in last dc: 10 Clusters.
Row 4: Ch 4, turn; sc in first Lace St, work Lace St,
sc in next Lace St, ★ 5 dc in Back Loop Only of next
sc, sc in next Lace St, (work Lace St, sc in next Lace St)
3 times, 5 dc in Back Loop Only of next sc, sc in next
Lace St, work Lace St, sc in next Lace St; repeat from ★
across to last sc, ch 1, dc in last sc: 18 5-dc groups.
Row 5: Ch 1, turn; sc in first dc, work Lace St, sc in
next Lace St, work Lace St, ★ work Cluster, work
Lace St, (sc in next Lace St, work Lace St) 3 times,
work Cluster, work Lace St, sc in next Lace St, work
Lace St; repeat from ★ across to last dc, sc in last dc:
18 Clusters.

Row 6: Ch 4, turn; sc in first Lace St, (work Lace St,
sc in next Lace St) twice, 5 dc in Back Loop Only of next
sc, sc in next Lace St, work Lace St, sc in next Lace St,
5 dc in Back Loop Only of next sc, sc in next Lace St,
★ (work Lace St, sc in next Lace St) 3 times, 5 dc in
Back Loop Only of next sc, sc in next Lace St, work
Lace St, sc in next Lace St, 5 dc in Back Loop Only of
next sc, sc in next Lace St; repeat from ★ across to last
2 Lace Sts, (work Lace St, sc in next Lace St) twice,
ch 1, dc in last sc: 18 5-dc groups.
Row 7: Ch 1, turn; sc in first dc, work Lace St, (sc in
next Lace St, work Lace St) twice, work Cluster, work
Lace St, sc in next Lace St, work Lace St, work Cluster,
work Lace St, ★ (sc in next Lace St, work Lace St) 3
times, work Cluster, work Lace St, sc in next Lace St,
work Lace St, work Cluster, work Lace St; repeat
from ★ across to last 2 Lace Sts, (sc in next Lace St,
work Lace St) twice, sc in last dc: 18 Clusters.
Row 8: Ch 4, turn; sc in first Lace St, (work Lace St,
sc in next Lace St) 3 times, 5 dc in Back Loop Only of
next sc, sc in next Lace St, ★ (work Lace St, sc in next
Lace St) 5 times, 5 dc in Back Loop Only of next sc, sc
in next Lace St; repeat from ★ across to last 3 Lace Sts,
(work Lace St, sc in next Lace St) 3 times, ch 1, dc in
last sc: 9 5-dc groups.
Row 9: Ch 1, turn; sc in first dc, work Lace St, (sc in
next Lace St, work Lace St) 3 times, work Cluster,
work Lace St, ★ (sc in next Lace St, work Lace St) 5
times, work Cluster, work Lace St; repeat from ★
across to last 3 Lace Sts, (sc in next Lace St, work
Lace St) 3 times, sc in last dc: 9 Clusters.
Rows 10 and 11: Repeat Rows 6 and 7.
Rows 12 and 13: Repeat Rows 4 and 5.
Rows 14-123: Repeat Rows 2-13, 9 times; then repeat
Rows 2 and 3 once **more**; do **not** finish off.

EDGING
Ch 1, working in end of rows, work Lace St, sc in first
row, (work Lace St, skip next row, sc in next row)
across; work Lace St, sc in free loop of first ch
(Fig. 19b, page 140), work Lace St, working over
beginning ch, (sc in next ch-3 sp, work Lace St) across
to last ch, sc in free loop of last ch; working in end of
rows, work Lace St, sc in first row, (work Lace St, skip
next row, sc in next row) across; working across last
row, work Lace St, sc in first sc, work Lace St, (sc in
next Lace St, work Lace St) across; join with slip st to
first st, finish off.

SPRING CLOVER

The combination of soft green and white clusters and stripes in this pretty cover-up will make you feel like you're lying in a field of clover.

Finished Size: Approximately 43″ x 55″

MATERIALS

Worsted Weight Yarn, approximately:
   Main Color (Green) - 17 ounces,
      (480 grams, 1,120 yards)
   Color A (Light Green) - 10 ounces,
      (280 grams, 660 yards)
   Color B (Dark Green) - 7 ounces,
      (200 grams, 460 yards)
   Color C (White) - 4 ounces, (110 grams, 265 yards)
Crochet hook, size H (5.00 mm) **or** size needed
   for gauge

GAUGE: In pattern, 3 Clusters and 12 rows = 6¼″

STRIPE SEQUENCE

2 Rows Color B, ★ (2 rows MC, 2 rows Color B) twice, (2 rows MC, 2 rows Color A) 3 times, (2 rows Color C, 2 rows Color A) 3 times, (2 rows MC, 2 rows Color A) twice, (2 rows MC, 2 rows Color B) 3 times; repeat from ★ once **more**.

PATTERN STITCHES

BEGINNING CLUSTER (uses first 4 sts)
Ch 3, ★ YO, insert hook in **next** st, YO and pull up a loop, YO and draw through 2 loops on hook; repeat from ★ 2 times **more**, YO and draw through all 4 loops on hook *(Figs. 9c & d, page 135)*.

CLUSTER (uses next 7 sts)
★ YO, insert hook in **next** st, YO and pull up a loop, YO and draw through 2 loops on hook; repeat from ★ 6 times **more**, YO and draw through all 8 loops on hook.

END CLUSTER (uses last 4 sts)
★ YO, insert hook in **next** st, YO and pull up a loop, YO and draw through 2 loops on hook; repeat from ★ 3 times **more**, YO and draw through all 5 loops on hook.

With Color B, ch 182 **loosely**.

Row 1 (Right side): Sc in second ch from hook and in each ch across: 181 sc.

Note: Loop a short piece of yarn around any stitch to mark last row as **right** side.

Row 2: Ch 1, turn; sc in first 2 sc, skip next 3 sc, 7 dc in next sc, (skip next 3 sc, sc in next 3 sc, skip next 3 sc, 7 dc in next sc) across to last 5 sc, skip next 3 sc, sc in last 2 sc; finish off: 18 7-dc groups.

Row 3: With **right** side facing, join yarn with slip st in first sc; work Beginning Cluster, ch 3, sc in next 3 dc, ch 3, (work Cluster, ch 3, sc in next 3 dc, ch 3) across to last 4 sts, work End Cluster: 19 Clusters.

Row 4: Ch 3, turn; 3 dc in same st, sc in next 3 sc, (7 dc in next Cluster, sc in next 3 sc) across to End Cluster, 4 dc in End Cluster; finish off: 17 7-dc groups.

Row 5: With **right** side facing, join yarn with slip st in first dc; sc in same st and in next dc, ch 3, work Cluster, ch 3, (sc in next 3 dc, ch 3, work Cluster, ch 3) across to last 2 dc, sc in last 2 dc: 18 Clusters.

Row 6: Ch 1, turn; sc in first 2 sc, 7 dc in next Cluster, (sc in next 3 sc, 7 dc in next Cluster) across to last 2 sc, sc in last 2 sc; finish off: 18 7-dc groups.

Rows 7-105: Repeat Rows 3-6, 24 times; then repeat Rows 3-5 once **more**.

Row 106: Ch 1, turn; sc in each st across; finish off: 181 sc.

Add tassels *(Figs. 24a & b, page 142)*.

PRETTY PANSIES

Blooming with rich color, this pretty afghan features a gardenful
of three-dimensional pansies — flowers known to symbolize
love and kind thoughts.

Finished Size: Approximately 48″ x 69″

MATERIALS
Worsted Weight Yarn, approximately:
  MC (Ecru) - 31 ounces, (880 grams, 1,950 yards)
  Color A (Green) - 5¼ ounces,
    (150 grams, 335 yards)
  Note: Yarn is needed for a total of 54 Motifs.
  Color B (assorted colors for Pansy petals) -
    ¼ ounce, (10 grams, 15 yards) for **each** Motif
  Color C (assorted colors for Pansy centers) -
    5 yards for **each** Motif
Crochet hooks, sizes F (3.75 mm) **and** J (6.00 mm) **or**
  sizes needed for gauge

GAUGE: With smaller size hook, one Square = 6¾″

SQUARE (Make 54)
With Color C and using smaller size hook, ch 4, join
with slip st to form a ring.
Rnd 1 (Right side): Ch 3 **(counts as first dc, now and
throughout)**, 2 dc in ring, ch 5, (3 dc in ring, ch 5) 4
times; join with slip st to first dc, finish off: 5 loops.
Rnd 2: With **right** side facing and using smaller size
hook, join Color B with slip st in center dc of any
3-dc group; ch 1, sc in same st, ★ in next loop work
[sc, ch 4, dc, ch 1, tr, ch 1, (dtr, ch 1) 7 times, tr, ch 1,
dc, ch 4, sc], sc in center dc of next 3-dc group; repeat
from ★ once **more**, (7 dc, ch 1, 7 dc) in next loop, [sc in
center dc of next 3-dc group, (7 dc, ch 1, 7 dc) in next
loop] twice; join with slip st to first sc: 5 petals.
Rnd 3: ★ Ch 3, (sc in next sp, ch 3) 12 times, skip next
sc, slip st in next sc; repeat from ★ once **more**, leave
remaining sts unworked.
Rnd 4: Ch 1, sc in same st, working **behind** petals,
ch 7, (sc in sc between next 2 petals, ch 7) twice, sc in
slip st between next 2 petals, ch 7, [sc in Back Loop
Only of center dtr on Rnd 2 of next petal *(Fig. 18,
page 140)*, ch 7] twice; join with slip st to first sc,
finish off: 6 loops.

Rnd 5: With **right** side facing and using larger size
hook, join Color A with slip st in both loops of first sc;
[ch 6 **loosely**, sc in second ch from hook, dc in next ch,
tr in last 3 chs **(leaf made)**], slip st in next loop, ch 3,
(working **behind** petals, slip st in next loop, work leaf)
twice, slip st in next sc, leave remaining sts unworked;
finish off.
Rnd 6: With **right** side facing, using larger size hook
and working **behind** leaves and petals, join MC with
slip st in first loop on Rnd 4; ch 1, sc in same sp, ch 6,
(sc in next loop, ch 6) around; join with slip st to first
sc: 6 loops.
Rnd 7: Slip st in first loop, ch 3, 7 dc in same sp, 8 dc in
next loop and in each loop around; join with slip st to
first dc: 48 dc.
Rnd 8: Ch 1, sc in same st and in each dc around; join
with slip st to first sc: 48 sc.
Rnd 9: Ch 1, sc in same st, ch 3, skip next sc, (sc in next
sc, ch 3, skip next sc) around; join with slip st to first sc:
24 ch-3 sps.
Rnd 10: Slip st in first ch-3 sp, ch 4, 6 tr in same sp, 3 dc
in next ch-3 sp, 2 sc in each of next 3 ch-3 sps, 3 dc in
next ch-3 sp, ★ 7 tr in next ch-3 sp, 3 dc in next ch-3 sp,
2 sc in each of next 3 ch-3 sps, 3 dc in next ch-3 sp;
repeat from ★ around; join with slip st to top of
beginning ch-6: 76 sts.
Rnd 11: Ch 1, sc in same st and in next 2 tr, 3 sc in next
tr, (sc in next 18 sts, 3 sc in next tr) 3 times, sc in last
15 sts; join with slip st to first sc, finish off: 84 sc.

JOINING
Note: Use larger size hook for Joining.
Afghan is assembled by joining 9 Squares into
6 vertical strips and then by joining strips.
Join Squares as follows: With **right** sides together and
working through Back Loop Only of **each** st on **both**
Squares, join MC with slip st in corner sc; slip st in next
21 sc; finish off.
Join strips in same manner.

EDGING

Note: Use larger size hook for Edging.

Rnd 1: With **right** side facing, working in Back Loops Only and working across long edge first, join MC with slip st in corner sc; ch 1, 3 sc in same st, ✝ sc in next 19 sc, hdc in next sc, dc in joining, hdc in next sc, (sc in next 18 sc, hdc in next sc, dc in joining, hdc in next sc) 7 times, sc in next 19 sc, 3 sc in next corner sc, sc in next 19 sc, hdc in next sc, dc in joining, hdc in next sc, (sc in next 18 sc, hdc in next sc, dc in joining, hdc in next sc) 4 times, sc in next 19 sc ✝, 3 sc in next sc, repeat from ✝ to ✝ once; join with slip st to first sc: 638 sts.

Rnd 2: Ch 1, sc in same st, 3 sc in next corner sc, ★ sc in next st and in each st across to next corner sc, 3 sc in corner sc; repeat from ★ 2 times **more**, sc in each st across; join with slip st to first sc: 646 sc.

Rnd 3: Ch 3, dc in next sc, 5 dc in next corner sc, ★ dc in each sc across to next corner sc, 5 dc in corner sc; repeat from ★ 2 times **more**, dc in each sc across; join with slip st to first dc, finish off.

Rnd 4: With **right** side facing, join Color A with slip st in any dc; ch 1, sc in same st, ch 2, skip next dc, (sc in next dc, ch 2, skip next dc) around; join with slip st to first sc, finish off.

Rnd 5: With **right** side facing, join MC with slip st in any ch-2 sp; ch 3, dc in same sp, 2 dc in next ch-2 sp and in each ch-2 sp around; join with slip st to first dc.

Rnd 6: Ch 1, sc in same st, ch 3, skip next dc, (sc in next dc, ch 3, skip next dc) around; join with slip st to first sc.

Rnd 7: Slip st in first ch-3 sp, ch 1, (sc, ch 3, sc) in same sp and in each ch-3 sp around; join with slip st to first sc, finish off.

PRECIOUS IN PINK

Precious in pink, this lacy afghan is perfect for a little baby girl. Graceful shells create a darling border.

Finished Size: Approximately 37″ x 37″

MATERIALS
Worsted Weight Yarn, approximately:
   16 ounces, (450 grams, 1,055 yards)
Crochet hook, size I (5.50 mm) **or** size needed for gauge

GAUGE: In pattern, 7 Clusters and 7 rows = 4″

PATTERN STITCHES
CLUSTER
YO, insert hook in **same** st, YO and pull up a loop, YO and draw through 2 loops on hook, skip next ch or dc, YO, insert hook in next st, YO and pull up a loop, YO and draw through 2 loops on hook, YO and draw through all 3 loops on hook *(Fig. 9c, page 135)*.
Note: Work last Cluster in same st as beginning ch-3 *(Fig. 9d, page 135)*.
SHELL
(2 Dc, ch 1, 2 dc) in stitch or space indicated.

Make a beginning loop as follows: Leaving a 3″ end, wind yarn around finger once to form a ring, YO and draw through ring *(Fig. 17, page 140)*. Work first round of stitches into ring and then pull end tightly to close ring.

Rnd 1 (Right side): Ch 4, dc in ring, ch 1, tr in ring, ch 1, ★ (dc in ring, ch 1) twice, tr in ring, ch 1; repeat from ★ 2 times **more**; join with slip st to third ch of beginning ch-4: 12 ch-1 sps.
Note: Loop a short piece of yarn around any stitch to mark last round as **right** side.

Rnd 2: Ch 3 **(counts as first dc, now and throughout)**, turn; (dc, ch 1, tr) in next tr **(first corner made)**, ch 1, ★ (work Cluster, ch 1) 3 times, tr in same st **(corner made)**, ch 1; repeat from ★ 2 times **more**, (work Cluster, ch 1) twice; join with slip st to **second** dc to form first Cluster: 3 Clusters **each** side.

Rnd 3: Ch 3, turn; dc in next Cluster, ch 1, (work Cluster, ch 1) twice, (dc, ch 1, tr, ch 1, dc) in same corner tr, ch 1, ★ (work Cluster, ch 1) 4 times, (dc, ch 1, tr, ch 1, dc) in same corner tr, ch 1; repeat from ★ 2 times **more**, work Cluster, ch 1; join with slip st to second dc: 4 Clusters **each** side.

Rnd 4: Ch 3, turn; dc in next Cluster, ch 1, ★ (work Cluster, ch 1) across and thru next corner tr, tr in same corner tr, ch 1; repeat from ★ 3 times **more**, (work Cluster, ch 1) across; join with slip st to second dc: 7 Clusters **each** side.

Rnd 5: Ch 3, turn; dc in next Cluster, ch 1, ★ (work Cluster, ch 1) across and thru next corner tr, (dc, ch 1, tr, ch 1, dc) in same corner tr, ch 1; repeat from ★ 3 times **more**, (work Cluster, ch 1) across; join with slip st to second dc: 8 Clusters **each** side.

Rnds 6-10: Repeat Rnds 4 and 5 twice, then repeat Rnd 4 once **more**: 19 Clusters **each** side.

Rnd 11: Ch 3, turn; ★ dc in next ch-1 sp, (dc in next Cluster, dc in next ch-1 sp) across to next corner tr, (2 dc, ch 2, 2 dc) in corner tr; repeat from ★ 3 times **more**, dc in next ch-1 sp, (dc in next Cluster, dc in next ch-1 sp) across; join with slip st to **first** dc: 43 dc **each** side.

Rnd 12: Ch 3, do **not** turn; (dc, ch 1, 2 dc) in same st, ch 1, ★ (skip next 4 dc, work Shell in next dc, ch 1) across to within 3 dc of next corner ch-2 sp, (3 dc, ch 2, 3 dc) in ch-2 sp, ch 1; repeat from ★ 3 times **more**, skip next 4 dc, (work Shell in next dc, ch 1, skip next 4 dc) across; join with slip st to first dc: 8 Shells **each** side.

Rnd 13: Slip st in next dc and in next ch-1 sp, ch 3, (dc, ch 1, 2 dc) in same sp, ch 1, ★ [work Shell in next Shell (ch-1 sp), ch 1] across to next corner ch-2 sp, work (Shell, ch 2, Shell) in ch-2 sp, ch 1; repeat from ★ 3 times **more**, (work Shell in next Shell, ch 1) across; join with slip st to first dc: 10 Shells **each** side.

Rnd 14: Slip st in next dc and in next ch-1 sp, ch 3, (dc, ch 1, 2 dc) in same sp, ch 1, ★ (work Shell in next Shell, ch 1) across to next corner ch-2 sp, (3 dc, ch 2, 3 dc) in ch-2 sp, ch 1; repeat from ★ 3 times **more**, (work Shell in next Shell, ch 1) across; join with slip st to first dc.

Rnd 15: Slip st in next dc and in next ch-1 sp, ch 3, (dc, ch 1, 2 dc) in same sp, ch 1, ★ (work Shell in next Shell, ch 1) across to next corner ch-2 sp, 2 dc in ch-2 sp, (ch 2, 2 dc) twice in same sp, ch 1; repeat from ★ 3 times **more**, (work Shell in next Shell, ch 1) across; join with slip st to first dc.

Rnd 16: Slip st in next dc and in next ch-1 sp, ch 3, (dc, ch 1, 2 dc) in same sp, ch 1, ★ (work Shell in next Shell, ch 1) across to next corner, work Shell in next ch-2 sp, ch 2, work Shell in next ch-2 sp, ch 1; repeat from ★ 3 times **more**, (work Shell in next Shell, ch 1) across; join with slip st to first dc: 12 Shells **each** side.

Rnd 17: Ch 3, dc in next dc, dc in next ch-1 sp, ★ (dc in next 2 dc, skip next ch-1 sp, dc in next 2 dc, dc in next ch-1 sp) across to within 2 dc of next corner ch-2 sp, dc in next 2 dc, 4 dc in next ch-2 sp, dc in next 2 dc, dc in next ch-1 sp; repeat from ★ 3 times **more**, (dc in next 2 dc, skip next ch-1 sp, dc in next 2 dc, dc in next ch-1 sp) across to last 2 dc, dc in last 2 dc; join with slip st to first dc: 256 dc.

Rnd 18: Slip st in next dc, ch 3, **turn**; skip next dc, dc in next dc, ch 1, (work Cluster, ch 1) 13 times, (dc, ch 1, tr, ch 1, dc) in same dc, ch 1, ★ (work Cluster, ch 1) 32 times, (dc, ch 1, tr, ch 1, dc) in same dc, ch 1; repeat from ★ 2 times **more**, (work Cluster, ch 1) across; join with slip st to **second** dc: 32 Clusters **each** side.

Rnds 19-26: Repeat Rnds 4 and 5, 4 times: 48 Clusters **each** side.

Rnd 27: Ch 3, turn; ★ dc in next ch-1 sp, (dc in next st, dc in next ch-1 sp) across to next corner tr, (dc, ch 2, dc) in corner tr; repeat from ★ 3 times **more**, dc in next ch-1 sp, (dc in next st, dc in next ch-1 sp) across; join with slip st to first dc: 103 dc **each** side.

Rnd 28: Do **not** turn; slip st in next 3 dc, ch 3, (dc, ch 1, 2 dc) in same st, ch 1, ★ (skip next 4 dc, work Shell in next dc, ch 1) across to within 3 dc of next corner ch-2 sp, (3 dc, ch 2, 3 dc) in ch-2 sp, ch 1; repeat from ★ 3 times **more**, skip next 4 dc, (work Shell in next dc, ch 1, skip next 4 dc) across; join with slip st to first dc: 20 Shells **each** side.

Rnds 29-32: Repeat Rnds 13-16: 24 Shells **each** side.

Rnd 33: Slip st in next dc and in next ch-1 sp, ch 3, 5 dc in same sp, ★ (sc in next ch-1 sp, 6 dc in next ch-1 sp) across to next corner ch-2 sp, (sc, ch 3, slip st in third ch from hook, sc) in ch-2 sp, 6 dc in next ch-1 sp; repeat from ★ 3 times **more**, sc in next ch-1 sp, (6 dc in next ch-1 sp, sc in next ch-1 sp) across; join with slip st to first dc, finish off.

RAMBLING ROSES

*Long-stemmed roses cascade down an openwork lattice pattern
on this elegant afghan reminiscent of yesteryear.*

MATERIALS
Worsted Weight Yarn, approximately:
  MC (Ecru) - 35 ounces, (1,000 grams, 2,230 yards)
  Color B (Rose) - 4 ounces, (110 grams, 255 yards)
  Color A (Green) - 8 ounces,
    (230 grams, 510 yards)
Crochet hook, size H (5.00 mm) **or** size needed for gauge
Yarn needle

Finished Size: Approximately 49″ x 64″

GAUGE: In pattern, 16 sts and 8 rows = 4″

With MC, ch 188 **loosely**.

Row 1 (Right side): Dc in sixth ch from hook, ★ ch 1, skip next ch, dc in next ch; repeat from ★ across: 92 ch-1 sps.

Row 2: Ch 4 **(counts as first dc plus ch 1, now and throughout)**, turn; dc in next dc, (dc in next ch-1 sp, dc in next dc) twice, ch 1, dc in next dc, ★ (dc in next ch-1 sp, dc in next dc) 4 times, ch 1, dc in next dc; repeat from ★ across to last 3 ch-1 sps, (dc in next ch-1 sp, dc in next dc) twice, ch 1, skip next ch, dc in next ch: 185 sts.

Row 3: Ch 4, turn; dc in next 4 dc, ch 1, dc in next ch-1 sp, ch 1, ★ skip next dc, dc in next 7 dc, ch 1, dc in next ch-1 sp, ch 1; repeat from ★ across to last 6 dc, skip next dc, dc in next 4 dc, ch 1, dc in last dc.

Row 4: Ch 4, turn; dc in next 3 dc, ch 1, dc in next ch-1 sp, dc in next dc, dc in next ch-1 sp, ch 1, ★ skip next dc, dc in next 5 dc, ch 1, dc in next ch-1 sp, dc in next dc, dc in next ch-1 sp, ch 1; repeat from ★ across to last 5 dc, skip next dc, dc in next 3 dc, ch 1, dc in last dc.

Row 5: Ch 4, turn; dc in next 2 dc, ch 1, dc in next ch-1 sp, dc in next 3 dc, dc in next ch-1 sp, ch 1, ★ skip next dc, dc in next 3 dc, ch 1, dc in next ch-1 sp, dc in next 3 dc, dc in next ch-1 sp, ch 1; repeat from ★ across to last 4 dc, skip next dc, dc in next 2 dc, ch 1, dc in last dc.

Row 6: Ch 4, turn; dc in next dc, ch 1, dc in next ch-1 sp, dc in next 5 dc, dc in next ch-1 sp, ch 1, skip next dc, dc in next dc, ch 1, ★ dc in next ch-1 sp, dc in next 5 dc, dc in next ch-1 sp, ch 1, skip next dc, dc in next dc, ch 1; repeat from ★ across to last ch-1 sp, dc in last dc.

Row 7: Ch 5 **(counts as first dc plus ch 2)**, turn; skip first ch-1 sp, dc in next ch-1 sp, dc in next 7 dc, dc in next ch-1 sp, ★ ch 1, dc in next ch-1 sp, dc in next 7 dc, dc in next ch-1 sp; repeat from ★ across to last 2 dc, ch 2, dc in last dc.

Row 8: Ch 4, turn; dc in first ch-2 sp, ch 1, skip next dc, dc in next 7 dc, ★ ch 1, dc in next ch-1 sp, ch 1, skip next dc, dc in next 7 dc; repeat from ★ across to last 2 dc, ch 1, dc in next ch-2 sp, ch 1, dc in last dc.

Row 9: Ch 4, turn; dc in next dc, ★ dc in next ch-1 sp, ch 1, skip next dc, dc in next 5 dc, ch 1, dc in next ch-1 sp, dc in next dc; repeat from ★ across to last dc, ch 1, dc in last dc.

Row 10: Ch 4, turn; dc in next 2 dc, dc in next ch-1 sp, ch 1, skip next dc, dc in next 3 dc, ch 1, dc in next ch-1 sp, ★ dc in next 3 dc, dc in next ch-1 sp, ch 1, skip next dc, dc in next 3 dc, ch 1, dc in next ch-1 sp; repeat from ★ across to last 3 dc, dc in next 2 dc, ch 1, dc in last dc.

Row 11: Ch 4, turn; dc in next 3 dc, dc in next ch-1 sp, ch 1, skip next dc, dc in next dc, ch 1, dc in next ch-1 sp, ★ dc in next 5 dc, dc in next ch-1 sp, ch 1, skip next dc, dc in next dc, ch 1, dc in next ch-1 sp; repeat from ★ across to last 4 dc, dc in next 3 dc, ch 1, dc in last dc.

Row 12: Ch 4, turn; dc in next 4 dc, dc in next ch-1 sp, ch 1, dc in next ch-1 sp, ★ dc in next 7 dc, dc in next ch-1 sp, ch 1, dc in next ch-1 sp; repeat from ★ across to last 5 dc, dc in next 4 dc, ch 1, dc in last dc.

Rows 13-122: Repeat Rows 3-12, 11 times.

Row 123: Ch 4, turn; dc in next dc, (ch 1, skip next dc, dc in next dc) twice, ch 1, dc in next dc, ★ (ch 1, skip next dc, dc in next dc) 4 times, ch 1, dc in next dc; repeat from ★ across to last 5 dc, (ch 1, skip next dc, dc in next dc) twice, ch 1, dc in last dc; do **not** finish off.

EDGING

Rnd 1: Ch 1, do **not** turn; working in end of rows, (sc, ch 2) twice in same sp, (sc in next sp, ch 2) across to next corner sp, ★ (sc, ch 2) 3 times in corner sp, (sc in next sp, ch 2) across to next corner sp; repeat from ★ around, sc in corner sp, ch 2; join with slip st to first sc, finish off.

Rnd 2: With **right** side facing, join Color B with slip st in any ch-2 sp; ch 1, insert hook in same sp and pull up a loop, insert hook in next ch-2 sp and pull up a loop, YO and draw through all 3 loops on hook, ch 3, ★ (insert hook in next ch-2 sp and pull up a loop) twice, YO and draw through all 3 loops on hook, ch 3; repeat from ★ around; join with slip st to first st, finish off.

Rnd 3: With **right** side facing, join Color A with slip st in any ch-3 sp; ch 3, 3 dc in same sp, (slip st, ch 3, 3 dc) in next ch-3 sp and in each ch-3 sp around; join with slip st to first st, finish off.

STEM (Make 2)

With Color A, work a ch 75" long; finish off.

ROSE (Make 14)

With Color B, ch 25 **loosely**.

Row 1: Dc in seventh ch from hook, (ch 2, skip next ch, dc in next ch) across: 10 ch-2 sps.

Row 2 (Right side): Ch 1, turn; (sc, 5 dc, sc) in first 8 ch-2 sps, (sc, 3 dc, sc) in last 2 sps; finish off leaving a 14" length for sewing.

Thread needle with yarn end. With **right** side facing and beginning with last petal made, roll Rose tightly, sewing through Row 1 as necessary to keep Rose secure.

LEAF (Make 42)

(Wrong side): With Color A, ch 5 **loosely**, sc in second ch from hook, hdc in next ch, dc in next ch, 5 dc in last ch; working in free loops of beginning ch **(Fig. 19b, page 140)**, dc in next ch, hdc in next ch, sc in next ch; join with slip st to first sc, finish off leaving a 10" length for sewing.

Referring to photo and Diagram for placement, sew Stems, Roses, and Leaves to afghan.

PLACEMENT DIAGRAM

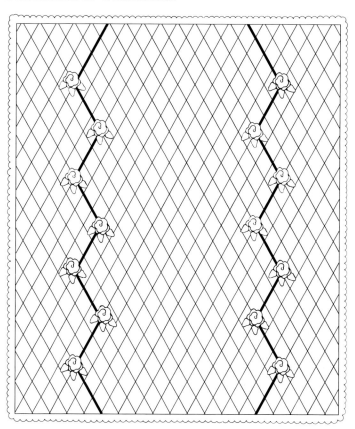

BABY-SOFT GRANNY

Granny squares in soft spring pastels are arranged in a diagonal pattern to create an afghan that's just precious for baby. Our join-as-you-go technique means there's no sewing required to finish this pretty project.

Finished Size: Approximately 36" x 45"

MATERIALS

Sport Weight Yarn, approximately:

MC (White) - 12 ounces, (340 grams, 1,200 yards)

Color A (Blue) - 3 ounces, (90 grams, 300 yards)

Color B (Green) - 3 ounces, (90 grams, 300 yards)

Color C (Pink) - 3 ounces, (90 grams, 300 yards)

Color D (Yellow) - 3 ounces, (90 grams, 300 yards)

Crochet hook, size D (3.25 mm) **or** size needed for gauge

GAUGE: One Square = 3" (point to point)

COLOR SEQUENCE			
	Rnd 1	**Rnd 2**	**Rnd 3**
◇1	B - Green	C - Pink	MC - White
◇2	A - Blue	D - Yellow	MC - White
◇3	C - Pink	B - Green	MC - White
◇4	D - Yellow	A - Blue	MC - White

Following Placement Chart, make Squares indicated using Color Sequence above.

FIRST SQUARE

Ch 4, join with slip st to form a ring.
Rnd 1 (Right side): Ch 3, 2 dc in ring, ch 2, (3 dc in ring, ch 2) 3 times; join with slip st to top of beginning ch-3, finish off: 4 ch-2 sps.
Note: Loop a short piece of yarn around any stitch to mark last round as **right** side.
Rnd 2: With **right** side facing, join yarn with slip st in any corner ch-2 sp; ch 3, (2 dc, ch 2, 3 dc) in same sp, ch 1, ★ (3 dc, ch 2, 3 dc) in next ch-2 sp, ch 1; repeat from ★ around; join with slip st to top of beginning ch-3, finish off: 8 sps.
Rnd 3: With **right** side facing, join MC with slip st in any corner ch-2 sp; ch 3, (2 dc, ch 2, 3 dc) in same sp, ch 1, 3 dc in next ch-1 sp, ch 1, ★ (3 dc, ch 2, 3 dc) in next ch-2 sp, ch 1, 3 dc in next ch-1 sp, ch 1; repeat from ★ around; join with slip st to top of beginning ch-3, finish off.

ADDITIONAL SQUARES

Ch 4, join with slip st to form a ring.
Rnds 1 and 2: Work same as First Square.
Rnd 3: Work One or Two Side Joining.

ONE SIDE JOINING

With **right** side facing, join MC with slip st in any corner ch-2 sp; ch 3, 2 dc in same sp, ch 1, holding Squares with **wrong** sides together, slip st in corner ch-2 sp on **previous Square**, ch 1, 3 dc in same ch-2 sp on **new Square**, ch 1, slip st in next ch-1 sp on **previous Square** *(Fig. 22, page 141)*, 3 dc in next ch-1 sp on **new Square**, ch 1, slip st in next ch-1 sp on **previous Square**, 3 dc in next ch-2 sp on **new Square**, ch 1, slip st in next ch-2 sp on **previous Square**, ch 1, 3 dc in same ch-2 sp on **new Square**, ch 1, 3 dc in next ch-1 sp, ch 1, ★ (3 dc, ch 2, 3 dc) in next ch-2 sp, ch 1, 3 dc in next ch-1 sp, ch 1; repeat from ★ around; join with slip st to top of beginning ch-3, finish off.

TWO SIDE JOINING

With **right** side facing, join MC with slip st in any corner ch-2 sp; ch 3, 2 dc in same sp, ch 1, holding Squares with **wrong** sides together, ★ slip st in corner ch-2 sp on **previous Square**, ch 1, 3 dc in same ch-2 sp on **new Square**, ch 1, slip st in next ch-1 sp on **previous Square**, 3 dc in next ch-1 sp on **new Square**, ch 1, slip st in next ch-1 sp on **previous Square**, 3 dc in next ch-2 sp on **new Square**, ch 1, slip st in next ch-2 sp on **previous Square**, ch 1; repeat from ★ once **more**, 3 dc in same ch-2 sp on **new Square**, ch 1, 3 dc in next ch-1 sp, ch 1, (3 dc, ch 2, 3 dc) in next ch-2 sp, ch 1, 3 dc in next ch-1 sp, ch 1; join with slip st to top of beginning ch-3, finish off.

EDGING

With **right** side facing, join MC with slip st in any corner ch-2 sp; ch 1, 3 sc in same sp, sc in each dc and in each ch-1 sp around, working 3 sc in each corner ch-2 sp; join with slip st to first sc, finish off.

PLACEMENT CHART

Row 1

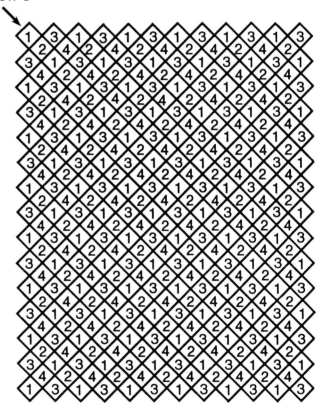

A PATCHWORK OF PETALS

*Because you hold two strands of yarn together
as you go, this floral afghan works up quickly.*

Finished Size: Approximately 47" x 65"

MATERIALS
Worsted Weight Yarn, approximately:
MC - 67 ounces, (1,910 grams, 4,265 yards)
CC (assorted colors) - ¼ ounce,
(10 grams, 16 yards) for **each** Square
Crochet hook, size N (10.00 mm) **or** size needed for
gauge

GAUGE: One Square = 4½"

Note: Entire afghan is worked holding two strands of
yarn together.

SQUARE (Make 117)

With CC ch 4, join with slip st to form a ring.
Rnd 1 (Right side): [Ch 3 **(counts as first dc, now and throughout)**, 3 dc in ring, drop loop from hook, insert hook in first dc, hook dropped loop and pull through **(beginning petal made)**], ch 2, ★ [4 dc in ring, drop loop from hook, insert hook in first dc of 4-dc group, hook dropped loop and pull through **(petal made)**], ch 2; repeat from ★ 4 times **more**; join with slip st to beginning petal, finish off: 6 petals.
Rnd 2: With **right** side facing, join MC with slip st in any ch-2 sp; ch 3, 3 dc in same sp, 4 dc in next ch-2 sp and in each ch-2 sp around; join with slip st to first dc: 24 dc.
Rnd 3: Ch 1, sc in same st, hdc in next dc, dc in next dc, (2 dc, ch 2, 2 dc) in next dc, dc in next dc, hdc in next dc, ★ sc in next dc, hdc in next dc, dc in next dc, (2 dc, ch 2, 2 dc) in next dc, dc in next dc, hdc in next dc; repeat from ★ around; join with slip st to first sc, finish off.

JOINING

Afghan is assembled by joining 13 Squares into 9 vertical strips and then by joining strips.
Join Squares as follows: With **wrong** sides together and working through inside loops of **each** st on **both** Squares, join MC with slip st in corner ch-2 sp; slip st in next 9 sts and in next corner ch-2 sp; finish off.
Join strips in same manner.

EDGING

Rnd 1: With **right** side facing, join MC with slip st in any corner ch-2 sp; ch 1, 3 sc in same sp, sc in BLO of next 9 sts *(Fig. 18, page 140)*, ★ (sc in next ch-2 sp, dc in joining between Squares, sc in next ch-2 sp, sc in BLO of next 9 sts) across to next corner ch-2 sp, 3 sc in corner sp, sc in BLO of next 9 sts; repeat from ★ 2 times **more**, (sc in next ch-2 sp, dc in joining between Squares, sc in next ch-2 sp, sc in BLO of next 9 sts) across; join with slip st to first sc.
Rnd 2: Ch 1, sc in same st, ch 3, skip next sc, (sc in next sc, ch 3, skip next st) around; join with slip st to first sc.
Rnd 3: Slip st in first ch-3 sp, ch 1, (sc, ch 3, sc) in same sp and in each ch-3 sp around; join with slip st to first sc, finish off.

WILDFLOWER WRAP

Light and airy as a springtime meadow, this blossoming wrap is as delicate as the wildflowers that inspired it.

Finished Size: Approximately 46" x 66"

MATERIALS

Worsted Weight Yarn, approximately:
Color A (Aqua) - 12 ounces,
(340 grams, 765 yards)
Color B (Rose) - 8 ounces, (230 grams, 510 yards)
Color C (Violet) - 8 ounces, (230 grams, 510 yards)
Color D (Blue) - 8 ounces, (230 grams, 510 yards)
Color E (Yellow) - 6 ounces, (170 grams, 385 yards)
Crochet hook, size H (5.00 mm) **or** size needed for gauge

GAUGE: One Flower = 5"

FIRST FLOWER

With Color E ch 6, join with slip st to form a ring.
Rnd 1 (Center - Right side): Ch 1, (sc in ring, ch 3) 12 times; join with slip st to first sc, finish off: 12 ch-3 sps.
Rnd 2: With **right** side facing, join Color A with slip st in any ch-3 sp; ch 1, sc in same sp, (ch 3, sc in next ch-3 sp) around, ch 1, hdc in first sc to form last sp: 12 ch-3 sps.
Rnd 3: Ch 1, sc in same sp, ch 6, sc in next ch-3 sp, (ch 3, sc in next ch-3 sp, ch 6, sc in next ch-3 sp) 5 times, ch 1, hdc in first sc to form last sp: 12 sps.
Rnd 4: Ch 1, sc in same sp, (5 dc, ch 3, 5 dc) in next ch-6 sp, ★ sc in next ch-3 sp, (5 dc, ch 3, 5 dc) in next ch-6 sp; repeat from ★ around; join with slip st to first sc, finish off.

ADDITIONAL FLOWERS

Work same as first Flower through Rnd 3, working Rnd 1 with Color E and additional rounds as indicated on Placement Chart.
Note: Flowers are joined as Rnd 4 is worked.
Join Flowers as follows: Holding **previous Flower** adjacent with **right** side facing, drop loop from hook and insert hook from front to back in corresponding ch-3 sp on **previous Flower**, hook dropped loop and pull through.
Rnd 4 (One Side Joining): Ch 1, sc in same sp, 5 dc in next ch-6 sp, ch 2, join Flowers, ch 1, 5 dc in same sp on new Flower, sc in next ch-3 sp, 5 dc in next ch-6 sp, ch 2, join Flowers, ch 1, 5 dc in same sp on new Flower, ★ sc in next ch-3 sp, (5 dc, ch 3, 5 dc) in next ch-6 sp; repeat from ★ around; join with slip st to first sc, finish off.

Referring to Diagram for placement and yarn color, work and join 11 **more** Flowers in the same manner to form a strip of 13 Flowers.
Work and join first Flower of next strip to first Flower of previous strip in the same manner, working in the joining where corners meet.
Work and join remaining Flowers in the same manner to assemble afghan as shown in Diagram, working in the joining where corners meet.

PLACEMENT CHART

KEY
A — Color A
B — Color B
C — Color C
D — Color D

EDGING

With **right** side facing and skipping all sc and joined ch-3 sps, join Color A with slip st in any corner ch-3 sp; ch 1, (sc, ch 3, sc) in same sp, sc in each dc across to next unattached ch-3 sp, ★ (sc, ch 3, sc) in ch-3 sp, sc in each dc across to next unattached ch-3 sp; repeat from ★ around; join with slip st to first sc, finish off.

TIMELESS BLUE AND WHITE

This quaint throw has the timeless charm of antique blue and white china. Featuring a progression of blues, the squares are bordered with a lacy edging.

Finished Size: Approximately 48″ x 60″

MATERIALS
Worsted Weight Yarn, approximately:
MC (Ecru) - 24 ounces, (680 grams, 1,580 yards)
Color A (Dark Blue) - 5 ounces,
   (140 grams, 330 yards)
Color B (Medium Blue) - 4 ounces,
   (110 grams, 265 yards)
Color C (Light Blue) - 4 ounces,
   (110 grams, 265 yards)
Crochet hook, size J (6.00 mm) **or** size needed for gauge

GAUGE: One Square = 6″

CLUSTER
★ YO, insert hook in stitch or space indicated, YO and pull up a loop, YO and draw through 2 loops on hook; repeat from ★ once **more**, YO and draw through all 3 loops on hook *(Figs. 9a & b, page 135)*.

SQUARE A (Make 17)
Color Sequence: 1 Rnd each of MC, Color A, Color B, MC, Color C, and MC.
Ch 8, join with slip st to form a ring.
Rnd 1 (Right side): Ch 1, 12 sc in ring; join with slip st to first sc, finish off: 12 sc.
Note: Loop a short piece of yarn around any stitch to mark last round as **right** side.
Rnd 2: With **right** side facing and working in Back Loops Only *(Fig. 18, page 140)*, join yarn with slip st in any sc; ch 2, dc in same st, ch 2, work Cluster in next sc, ch 4 (corner), work Cluster in next sc, ★ (ch 2, work Cluster in next sc) twice, ch 4 (corner), work Cluster in next sc; repeat from ★ around, ch 2; join with slip st to **both** loops of first dc, finish off: 12 sps.
Rnd 3: With **right** side facing, join yarn with slip st in any corner ch-4 sp; ch 1, (sc, ch 6, sc) in same sp, ch 4, (sc in next ch-2 sp, ch 4) twice, ★ (sc, ch 6, sc) in next corner ch-4 sp, ch 4, (sc in next ch-2 sp, ch 4) twice; repeat from ★ around, cut yarn; join next color with slip st to first sc: 16 sps.

Rnd 4: Ch 1, ★ (sc, ch 6, sc) in next corner ch-6 sp, (sc, ch 3, sc) in each of next 3 sps; repeat from ★ around, cut yarn; join next color with slip st to first sc.
Rnd 5: Slip st in first corner ch-6 sp, ch 2, dc in same sp, ch 2, work (tr, ch 3, tr, ch 2, Cluster) in same sp, work (Cluster, ch 1, Cluster) in each of next 3 ch-3 sps, ★ work (Cluster, ch 2, tr, ch 3, tr, ch 2, Cluster) in next corner ch-6 sp, work (Cluster, ch 1, Cluster) in each of next 3 ch-3 sps; repeat from ★ around, cut yarn; join next color with slip st to first dc: 24 sps.
Rnd 6: Ch 1, (sc, ch 2, sc) in first ch-2 sp, ch 1, (sc, ch 5, sc) in next corner ch-3 sp, ch 1, ★ [(sc, ch 2, sc) in next sp, ch 1] 5 times, (sc, ch 5, sc) in next corner ch-3 sp, ch 1; repeat from ★ 2 times **more**, [(sc, ch 2, sc) in next sp, ch 1] 4 times; join with slip st to first sc, finish off.

SQUARE B (Make 18)
Color Sequence: 1 Rnd each of Color C, MC, Color B, MC, Color A, and MC.
Work same as Square A.

SQUARE C (Make 28)
Color Sequence: 1 Rnd each of Color A, MC, Color B, 3 rnds of MC.
Work same as Square A through Rnd 3.
Rnd 4: Ch 1, ★ (sc, ch 6, sc) in next corner ch-6 sp, (sc, ch 3, sc) in each of next 3 sps; repeat from ★ around; join with slip st to first sc.
Rnd 5: Slip st in first corner ch-6 sp, ch 2, dc in same sp, ch 2, work (tr, ch 3, tr, ch 2, Cluster) in same sp, work (Cluster, ch 1, Cluster) in each of next 3 ch-3 sps, ★ work (Cluster, ch 2, tr, ch 3, tr, ch 2, Cluster) in next corner ch-6 sp, work (Cluster, ch 1, Cluster) in each of next 3 ch-3 sps; repeat from ★ around; join with slip st to first dc: 24 sps.
Rnd 6: Ch 1, (sc, ch 2, sc) in first ch-2 sp, ch 1, (sc, ch 5, sc) in next corner ch-3 sp, ch 1, ★ [(sc, ch 2, sc) in next sp, ch 1] 5 times, (sc, ch 5, sc) in next corner ch-3 sp, ch 1; repeat from ★ 2 times **more**, [(sc, ch 2, sc) in next sp, ch 1] 4 times; join with slip st to first sc, finish off.

ASSEMBLY

Afghan is assembled by joining 9 Squares into 7 vertical strips and then by joining strips.
Note: Refer to Placement Chart, page 33.

SQUARE JOINING

Holding two Squares with **wrong** sides together and working through **both** Squares, join MC with slip st in corner ch-5 sp; ch 1, sc in same sp, (ch 2, skip next ch-1 sp, sc in next ch-2 sp) 5 times, ch 2, skip next ch-1 sp, (sc, ch 1, slip st) in next corner ch-5 sp; finish off.
Repeat for remaining Squares.

STRIP JOINING

Holding two Strips with **wrong** sides together and working through **both** Strips, join MC with slip st in first corner ch-5 sp; ch 1, sc in same sp, (ch 2, skip next ch-1 sp, sc in next ch-2 sp) 5 times, ch 2, skip next ch-1 sp, ★ sc in next corner ch-5 sp, ch 2, sc in corner ch-5 sp on **next** Square, (ch 2, skip next ch-1 sp, sc in next ch-2 sp) 5 times, ch 2, skip next ch-1 sp; repeat from ★ across to last corner ch-5 sp, (sc, ch 1, slip st) in corner ch-5 sp; finish off.
Repeat for remaining Strips, always working in same direction.

EDGING

Rnd 1: With **right** side facing, join MC with slip st in any corner ch-5 sp of Afghan, loop a short piece of yarn around this ch-5 to mark Ridge placement; ch 1, sc in same sp, ch 3, (skip next ch-1 sp, sc in next ch-2 sp, ch 3) 5 times, skip next ch-1 sp, sc in next corner ch-5 sp, † ch 3, sc in corner ch-5 sp of **next** Square, ch 3, (skip next ch-1 sp, sc in next ch-2 sp, ch 3) 5 times, skip next ch-1 sp, sc in next corner ch-5 sp †, repeat from † to † across through next corner of Afghan, ★ ch 5, sc in same corner sp, ch 3, (skip next ch-1 sp, sc in next ch-2 sp, ch 3) 5 times, skip next ch-1 sp, sc in next corner ch-5 sp, repeat from † to † across through next corner of Afghan; repeat from ★ 2 times **more**, ch 2, dc in first sc to form last loop.

Rnd 2: Ch 1, (sc, ch 5, sc) in same sp, ch 3, (sc in next ch-3 sp, ch 3) across to next corner ch-5 sp, ★ (sc, ch 5, sc) in corner sp, ch 3, (sc in next ch-3 sp, ch 3) across to next corner ch-5 sp; repeat from ★ around; join with slip st to first sc.

Rnd 3: Slip st in first corner ch-5 sp, ch 2, work (dc, ch 7, Cluster) in same sp, ch 2, (work Cluster in next ch-3 sp, ch 2) across to next corner ch-5 sp, ★ work (Cluster, ch 7, Cluster) in corner sp, ch 2, (work Cluster in next ch-3 sp, ch 2) across to next corner ch-5 sp; repeat from ★ around; join with slip st to first dc, finish off.

Rnd 4: With **right** side facing, join Color C with slip st in any corner ch-7 loop; ch 1, (sc, ch 6, sc) in same loop, ch 4, (sc in next ch-2 sp, ch 4) across to next corner ch-7 loop, ★ (sc, ch 6, sc) in corner loop, ch 4, (sc in next ch-2 sp, ch 4) across to next corner ch-7 loop; repeat from ★ around; join with slip st to first sc, finish off.

Rnd 5: With **right** side facing, join MC with slip st in any corner ch-6 loop; ch 1, (sc, ch 6, sc) in same sp, (sc, ch 3, sc) in each sp across to next corner ch-6 loop, ★ (sc, ch 6, sc) in corner loop, (sc, ch 3, sc) in each sp across to next corner ch-6 loop; repeat from ★ around; join with slip st to first sc.

Rnd 6: Slip st in first corner sp, ch 2, work (dc, ch 2, tr, ch 3, tr, ch 2, Cluster) in same loop, work (Cluster, ch 1, Cluster) in each sp across to next corner ch-6 loop, ★ work (Cluster, ch 2, tr, ch 3, tr, ch 2, Cluster) in corner ch-6 loop, work (Cluster, ch 1, Cluster) in each sp across to next corner ch-6 loop; repeat from ★ around; join with slip st to first dc, finish off.

Rnd 7: With **right** side facing, join Color A with slip st in any corner ch-3 sp; ch 1, (sc, ch 5, sc) in same sp, ch 1, (sc, ch 3, sc) in each sp across to next corner ch-3 sp, ch 1, ★ (sc, ch 5, sc) in corner ch-3 sp, ch 1, (sc, ch 3, sc) in each sp across to next corner ch-3 sp, ch 1; repeat from ★ around; join with slip st to first sc, finish off.

BRIDGE

With **right** side of Afghan facing, join MC with slip st in third ch of marked ch-5, ch 2; fold Edging back; working over last round of Squares **and** first round of Edging, sc in same corner loop, ch 2, (skip next ch-1 sp, sc in next ch-2 sp, ch 2) 5 times, skip next ch-1 sp, sc in next corner ch-5 sp, † ch 2, sc in corner ch-5 sp of **next** Square, ch 2, (skip next ch-1 sp, sc in next ch-2 sp, ch 2) 5 times, skip next ch-1 sp, sc in next corner ch-5 sp †, repeat from † to † across through next corner of Afghan, ★ ch 2, slip st in third ch of ch-5 loop, ch 2, sc in same corner loop, ch 2, (skip next ch-1 sp, sc in next ch-2 sp, ch 2) 5 times, skip next ch-1 sp, sc in next corner ch-5 sp, repeat from † to † across through next corner of Afghan; repeat from ★ 2 times **more**, ch 2; join with slip st to first slip st, finish off.

Square A   Square B   Square C

PLACEMENT CHART

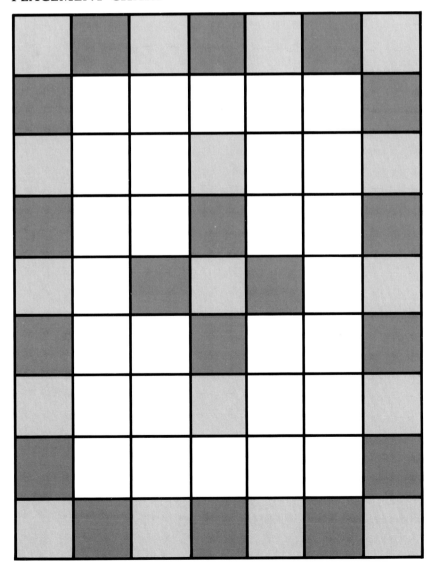

SOFT AND FEMININE

Soft and feminine, this lacy shell afghan will make a pretty addition to your bedroom. Because you work with two strands of yarn held together, it's extra easy and quick to finish.

Finished Size: Approximately 46" x 70"

MATERIALS
   Worsted Weight Yarn, approximately:
      62 ounces, (1,760 grams, 3,900 yards)
   Crochet hook, size P (12.00 mm) **or** size needed for
      gauge

GAUGE: In pattern, (Shell, sc) twice and 6 rows = 4½"

Note: Entire afghan is worked holding two strands of yarn together.

Ch 119 **loosely**.
Row 1: Sc in eighth ch from hook, ch 2, skip next 2 chs, dc in next ch, ★ ch 2, skip next 2 chs, sc in next ch, ch 2, skip next 2 chs, dc in next ch; repeat from ★ across: 38 sps.

Row 2 (Right side): Ch 1, turn; sc in first dc, 5 dc in next sc, (sc in next dc, 5 dc in next sc) across, skip next 2 chs, sc in next ch: 19 5-dc group.
Row 3: Ch 5, turn; sc in center dc of next 5-dc group, ch 2, dc in next sc, ★ ch 2, sc in center dc of next 5-dc group, ch 2, dc in next sc; repeat from ★ across: 38 ch-2 sps.
Rows 4-89: Repeat Rows 2 and 3, 43 times; do **not** finish off.

EDGING

Rnd 1: Ch 1, turn; 3 sc in first dc, 2 sc in next ch-2 sp, sc in next sc, ★ 2 sc in next ch-2 sp, sc in next dc, 2 sc in next ch-2 sp, sc in next sc; repeat from ★ across to last sp, 2 sc in last sp, 3 sc in corner ch; working in end of rows, 2 sc in end of same row and in each row across; working in free loops of beginning ch *(Fig. 19b, page 140)*, 3 sc in corner ch (third ch before next sc), sc in each ch across to last ch, 3 sc in last ch; working in end of rows, 2 sc in end of same row and in each row across; join with slip st to first sc: 594 sc.
Rnd 2: Ch 1, sc in first sc, skip next 2 sc, 7 dc in next sc, skip next 2 sc, ★ sc in next sc, skip next 2 sc, 7 dc in next sc, skip next 2 sc; repeat from ★ around; join with slip st to first sc, finish off.

SUMMER

All the things we love best about summer — clear blue skies, delightful daisies, and bright red watermelons — prompted us to create this sunny collection of afghans. There are lots of pretty throws to enhance your summertime fun — and keep your fingers busy, too! Whether you make one to spread out for a picnic or to celebrate the Fourth of July, you're sure to find just the right pattern on the following pages.

JUST FOR "EWE"

*Designed especially for "ewe," this playful afghan features
popcorn stitches arranged to resemble dominoes.*

Finished Size: Approximately 52″ x 72″

MATERIALS
   Worsted Weight Yarn, approximately:
      67 ounces, (1,900 grams, 4,560 yards)
   Crochet hook, size H (5.00 mm) **or** size needed for
   gauge

GAUGE: In pattern, 14 sc and 15 rows = 4″

POPCORN
Work 5 dc in next sc, drop loop from hook, insert
hook in first dc of 5-dc group, hook dropped loop and
draw through *(Fig. 12, page 137)*, ch 1 to close.

Ch 252 **loosely**.
Row 1 (Right side): Sc in second ch from hook and in
each ch across: 251 sc.
**Row 2 AND ALL WRONG SIDE ROWS
through Row 10:** Ch 1, turn; sc in each st across.
Row 3: Ch 1, turn; sc in first 2 sc, work Popcorn, (sc in
next 2 sc, work Popcorn) twice, ★ sc in next 14 sc, work
Popcorn, (sc in next 2 sc, work Popcorn) twice; repeat
from ★ 10 times **more**, sc in last 11 sc: 36 Popcorns.

Row 5: Ch 1, turn; sc in first 14 sc, work Popcorn, (sc
in next 20 sc, work Popcorn) 11 times, sc in last 5 sc:
12 Popcorns.
Row 7: Ch 1, turn; sc in first 11 sc, work Popcorn, sc in
next 5 sc, work Popcorn, ★ sc in next 14 sc, work
Popcorn, sc in next 5 sc, work Popcorn; repeat from ★
10 times **more**, sc in last 2 sc: 24 Popcorns.
Row 9: Repeat Row 5.
Row 11: Repeat Row 3.
Rows 12-14: Ch 1, turn; sc in each st across.
Row 15: Ch 3 **(counts as first dc, now and
throughout)**, turn; dc in next 2 sc, (ch 1, skip next sc, dc
in next 3 sc) across: 62 ch-1 sps.
Row 16: Ch 1, turn; sc in first 3 dc and in first ch-1 sp,
(ch 3 **loosely**, sc in next ch-1 sp) across to last 3 dc, sc in
last 3 dc: 61 ch-3 sps.
Row 17: Ch 3, turn; dc in next 2 sc, ch 1, (skip next sc,
3 dc in next ch-3 sp, ch 1) across to last 4 sc, skip next
sc, dc in last 3 sc: 62 ch-1 sps.
Row 18: Ch 1, turn; sc in each dc and in each ch-1 sp
across: 251 sc.
Rows 19 and 20: Ch 1, turn; sc in each sc across.
Row 21: Ch 1, turn; sc in first 11 sc, work Popcorn,
(sc in next 2 sc, work Popcorn) twice, ★ sc in next 14 sc,
work Popcorn, (sc in next 2 sc, work Popcorn) twice;
repeat from ★ 10 times **more**, sc in last 2 sc:
36 Popcorns.
**Row 22 AND ALL WRONG SIDE ROWS
through Row 28:** Ch 1, turn; sc in each st across.
Row 23: Ch 1, turn; sc in first 5 sc, work Popcorn, (sc
in next 20 sc, work Popcorn) 11 times, sc in last 14 sc:
12 Popcorns.
Row 25: Ch 1, turn; sc in first 2 sc, work Popcorn, sc in
next 5 sc, work Popcorn, ★ sc in next 14 sc, work
Popcorn, sc in next 5 sc, work Popcorn; repeat from ★
10 times **more**, sc in last 11 sc: 24 Popcorns.
Row 27: Repeat Row 23.
Row 29: Repeat Row 21.
Rows 30-38: Repeat Rows 12-20.
Rows 39-193: Repeat Rows 3-38, 4 times; then repeat
Rows 3-13 once **more**.
Finish off.

Add fringe *(Figs. 25a & b, page 142)*.

PERFECT FOR THE PORCH

Crocheted in the colors of old roses and blue summer skies, this granny square variation is perfect for the front porch.

Finished Size: Approximately 53" x 68"

MATERIALS

Worsted Weight Yarn, approximately:
- MC (Dark Rose) - 20½ ounces,
  (580 grams, 1,290 yards)
- Color A (Ecru) - 7½ ounces,
  (220 grams, 470 yards)
- Color B (Light Blue) - 12 ounces,
  (340 grams, 755 yards)
- Color C (Dark Blue) - 11½ ounces,
  (330 grams, 725 yards)
- Crochet hook, size I (5.50 mm) **or** size needed for gauge
- Yarn needle

GAUGE: One Small Square = 3¾"

CLUSTER

★ YO, insert hook in stitch indicated, YO and pull up a loop, YO and draw through 2 loops on hook; repeat from ★ 2 times **more**, YO and draw through all 4 loops on hook *(Figs. 9a & b, page 135)*.

SMALL SQUARE (Make 48)

With Color A ch 4, join with slip st to form a ring.

Rnd 1 (Right side)**:** Ch 1, (sc, ch 1, dc, ch 1) 4 times in ring; join with slip st to first sc: 8 ch-1 sps.

Note: Loop a short piece of yarn around any stitch to mark last round as **right** side.

Rnd 2: Ch 1, turn; sc in first ch-1 sp, ch 3, sc in next ch-1 sp, work Cluster in Back Loop Only *(Fig. 18, page 140)* of next sc, ★ sc in next ch-1 sp, ch 3, sc in next ch-1 sp, work Cluster in Back Loop Only of next sc; repeat from ★ around; join with slip st to first sc, finish off: 4 Clusters.

Rnd 3: With **right** side facing, join Color B with slip st in any ch-3 sp; ch 3 **(counts as first dc, now and throughout)**, (2 dc, ch 3, 3 dc) in same sp, ch 1, ★ (3 dc, ch 3, 3 dc) in next ch-3 sp, ch 1; repeat from ★ around; join with slip st to first dc, finish off.

Rnd 4: With **right** side facing, join MC with slip st in any ch-3 sp; ch 3, (2 dc, ch 3, 3 dc) in same sp, ch 1, 3 dc in next ch-1 sp, ch 1, ★ (3 dc, ch 3, 3 dc) in next ch-3 sp, ch 1, 3 dc in next ch-1 sp, ch 1; repeat from ★ around; join with slip st to first dc, finish off.

CORNER SQUARE (Make 4)

Work same as Small Square working Rnd 3 with Color C.

BAR (Make 60)

Foundation Chain (Wrong side)**:** With Color A, (ch 3, work Cluster in second ch from hook) 5 times, ch 2; finish off: 5 Clusters (5").

Note: Mark opposite side as **right** side.

Rnd 1: With **right** side facing and working in ch **between** Clusters on foundation chain, join Color B with slip st in ch between first 2 Clusters; ch 3, 2 dc in same ch, ch 1, (3 dc in next ch, ch 1) across, 3 dc in last ch, (ch 3, 3 dc) twice in same ch, ch 1; working in free loops of chs between Clusters on second side of Foundation chain, (3 dc in next ch, ch 1) across, 3 dc in last ch, (ch 3, 3 dc) twice in same ch, ch 1; join with slip st to first dc, finish off.

Rnd 2: With **right** side facing and holding Bar vertically, join Color C with slip st in top **right** ch-3 sp; ch 3, (2 dc, ch 3, 3 dc) in same sp, ch 1, (3 dc, ch 3, 3 dc) in next ch-3 sp, ch 1, (3 dc in next ch-1 sp, ch 1) across to next ch-3 sp, [(3 dc, ch 3, 3 dc) in next ch-3 sp, ch 1] twice, (3 dc in next ch-1 sp, ch 1) across; join with slip st to first dc, finish off.

Rnd 3: With **right** side facing and holding Bar vertically, join MC with slip st in top **right** ch-3 sp; ch 3, (2 dc, ch 3, 3 dc) in same sp, ch 1, 3 dc in next ch-1 sp, ch 1, (3 dc, ch 3, 3 dc) in next ch-3 sp, ch 1, (3 dc in next ch-1 sp, ch 1) across to next ch-3 sp, (3 dc, ch 3, 3 dc) in ch-3 sp, ch 1, 3 dc in next ch-1 sp, ch 1, (3 dc, ch 3, 3 dc) in next ch-3 sp, ch 1, (3 dc in next ch-1 sp, ch 1) across; join with slip st to first dc, finish off.

LONG BORDER STRIP (Make 2)

Foundation Chain (Wrong side)**:** With Color A, (ch 3, work Cluster in second ch from hook) 56 times, ch 2; finish off: 56 Clusters (56").

Note: Mark opposite side as **right** side.

Rnds 1-3: Work same as Bar in the following color sequence: One round **each** of Color C, Color B, and MC.

SHORT BORDER STRIP (Make 2)

Foundation Chain (Wrong side)**:** With Color A, (ch 3, work Cluster in second ch from hook) 41 times, ch 2; finish off: 41 Clusters (41").

Note: Mark opposite side as **right** side.

Rnds 1-3: Work same as Bar in the following color sequence: One round **each** of Color C, Color B, and MC.

JOINING

Note: When whipstitching strips together, use MC, always begin at the same end, and work through both loops *(Fig. 23a, page 141)*.

Afghan is assembled by whipstitching 5 Bars and 4 Small Squares into 12 vertical strips, and then by whipstitching strips together. Whipstitch Short Border Strips to ends of Afghan. Whipstitch a Corner Square to each end of each Long Border Strip, then whipstitch to sides of Afghan.

PLACEMENT CHART

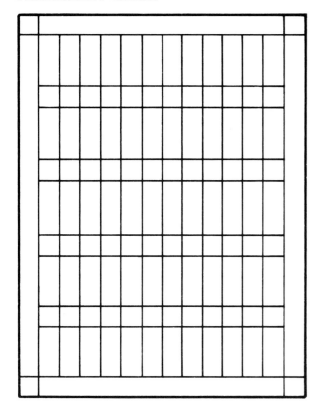

EDGING

Rnd 1: With **right** side facing, join MC with sc *(see Joining with Sc, page 140)* in any corner ch-3 sp; ch 2, sc in same sp, ★ † ch 1, skip next dc, sc in next dc, ch 1, (sc in next ch-1 sp, ch 1, skip next dc, sc in next dc, ch 1) twice, (sc in next sp, ch 1) twice, skip next dc, sc in next dc, ch 1, (sc in next ch-1 sp, ch 1, skip next dc, sc in next dc, ch 1) across to next Corner Square, (sc in next sp, ch 1) twice, skip next dc, sc in next dc, ch 1, (sc in next ch-1 sp, ch 1, skip next dc, sc in next dc, ch 1) twice †, (sc, ch 2, sc) in next corner ch-3 sp; repeat from ★ 2 times **more**, then repeat from † to † once; join with slip st to first sc.

Rnd 2: (Ch 1, slip st) twice in first ch-2 sp, (ch 1, slip st in next ch-1 sp) across to next ch-2 sp, ★ (ch 1, slip st) twice in ch-2 sp, (ch 1, slip st in next ch-1 sp) across to next ch-2 sp; repeat from ★ around; join with slip st to first st, finish off.

QUILT-BLOCK FLOWERS

Trimmed with a colorful edging of flowers, this pretty throw has all the charm of an antique quilt. Its patchwork-look blocks of rosy blooms evoke images of lazy summer afternoons spent picking flowers.

Finished Size: Approximately 56" x 71"

MATERIALS
Worsted Weight Yarn, approximately:
  MC (White) - 27 ounces, (770 grams, 1,775 yards)
  Color A (Green) - 10 ounces,
    (280 grams, 660 yards)
  Color B (Light Green) - 5 ounces,
    (140 grams, 330 yards)
  Color C (Rose) - 11 ounces, (310 grams, 725 yards)
  Color D (Light Rose) - 9 ounces,
    (260 grams, 595 yards)
Crochet hook, size I (5.50 mm) **or** size needed for
  gauge
Yarn needle

GAUGE: 4 Blocks = 4"
    Rows 1-5 = 4" x 4" x 5½" (triangle)
    Each Square = 7½"

PATTERN STITCHES
BEGINNING BLOCK
Ch 5, turn; 3 dc in fourth ch from hook.
BLOCK
Slip st in ch-3 sp of next Block, ch 3, 3 dc in same sp, unless otherwise instructed.

SQUARE (Make 48)
Note: Square is worked diagonally, from corner to corner.
Row 1 (Right side): With Color A ch 5, 3 dc in fifth ch from hook **(First Block made)**.
Note #1: Loop a short piece of yarn around any stitch to mark last row as **right** side.
Note #2: See Symbol Crochet Chart, page 139, for illustration of Rows 1-7.
Note #3: When changing colors **(Fig. 21, page 141)**, keep unused color to **wrong** side of work; do **not** cut yarn until color is no longer needed. Do not carry colors on wrong side of work; use a separate skein or ball for each color change.
Row 2: Work Beginning Block, slip st around beginning ch of previous Block **(Fig. 16a, page 139)**, ch 3, 3 dc in same sp **(Fig. 16b, page 139)**, changing to MC in last dc: 2 Blocks.

Row 3: Work Beginning Block; with Color A, slip st in ch-3 sp of first Block, ch 3, 3 dc in same sp; with MC, work last Block: 3 Blocks.
Row 4: Work Beginning Block; with Color A, slip st in ch-3 sp of first Block, ch 3, 3 dc in same sp, work Block; with MC, work last Block: 4 Blocks.
Row 5: Work Beginning Block; with Color A, slip st in ch-3 sp of first Block, ch 3, 3 dc in same sp; with Color B, work Block; with Color A, work Block; with MC, work last Block: 5 Blocks.
Row 6: Work Beginning Block, slip st in ch-3 sp of first Block, ch 3, 3 dc in same sp; with Color B, work 2 Blocks; with MC, work 2 Blocks: 6 Blocks.
Row 7: Work Beginning Block, slip st in ch-3 sp of first Block, ch 3, 3 dc in same sp; with Color B, work 3 Blocks; with MC, work 2 Blocks: 7 Blocks.
Row 8: Work Beginning Block, slip st in ch-3 sp of first Block, ch 3, 3 dc in same sp; with Color C, work 4 Blocks; with MC, work 2 Blocks: 8 Blocks.
Row 9: Work Beginning Block, slip st in ch-3 sp of first Block, ch 3, 3 dc in same sp; with Color C, work 2 Blocks; with Color D, work Block; with Color C, work 2 Blocks; with MC, work 2 Blocks: 9 Blocks.
Row 10: Work Beginning Block, slip st in ch-3 sp of first Block, ch 3, 3 dc in same sp; with Color C, work 2 Blocks; with Color D, work 2 Blocks; with Color C, work 2 Blocks; with MC, work 2 Blocks: 10 Blocks.
Row 11: Turn; slip st in first 3 dc and in first ch-3 sp, ch 3, 3 dc in same sp; with Color C, work 2 Blocks; with Color D, work 3 Blocks; with Color C, work 2 Blocks; with MC, work Block, slip st in ch-3 sp of last Block: 9 Blocks.
Row 12: Turn; slip st in first 3 dc and in first ch-3 sp, ch 3, 3 dc in same sp, work Block; with Color D, work 4 Blocks; with MC, work 2 Blocks, slip st in ch-3 sp of last Block: 8 Blocks.
Row 13: Turn; slip st in first 3 dc and in first ch-3 sp, ch 3, 3 dc in same sp, work 2 Blocks; with Color C, work Block; with MC, work 3 Blocks, slip st in ch-3 sp of last Block: 7 Blocks.
Rows 14-17: Turn; slip st in first 3 dc and in first ch-3 sp, ch 3, 3 dc in same sp, work Blocks across to last Block, slip st in ch-3 sp of last Block: 3 Blocks.

Row 18: Turn; slip st in first 3 dc and in first ch-3 sp, ch 3, 3 dc in same sp, work Block, slip st in ch-3 sp of last Block: 2 Blocks.

Row 19: Turn; slip st in first 3 dc and in first ch-3 sp, ch 3, 3 dc in same sp, slip st in ch-3 sp of last Block; finish off.

JOINING

Using Placement Chart as a guide, whipstitch 4 Squares into one Large Block working through one strand of each piece *(Fig. 23a, page 141)*. Join remaining Squares in same manner.

Whipstitch 4 Large Blocks into 3 vertical strips, then whipstitch strips together.

PLACEMENT CHART

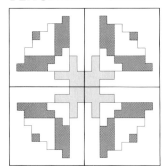

BORDER

Foundation Round: With **right** side facing, join Color A with slip st in ch-3 sp of any corner Block; ch 3, 3 dc in same sp, (skip next 3 dc, work Block) 5 times, skip next dc, work Block in next dc, skip next dc, work Block, ★ (skip next 3 dc, work Block) 4 times, skip next dc, work Block in next dc, skip next dc, work Block; repeat from ★ 25 times **more**, (skip next 3 dc, work Block) 3 times, skip next dc, work Block in next dc, skip last dc, slip st in same sp as first Block; do **not** finish off: 168 Blocks.

FIRST TRIANGLE

Row 1: Turn; slip st in first 3 dc and in first ch-3 sp, ch 3, 3 dc in same sp, work 4 Blocks, slip st in ch-3 sp of next Block: 5 Blocks.

Row 2: Turn; slip st in first 3 dc and in first ch-3 sp, ch 3, 3 dc in same sp, work 3 Blocks, slip st in ch-3 sp of last Block: 4 Blocks.

Row 3: Turn; slip st in first 3 dc and in first ch-3 sp, ch 3, 3 dc in same sp, work 2 Blocks, slip st in ch-3 sp of last Block: 3 Blocks.

Row 4: Turn; slip st in first 3 dc and in first ch-3 sp, ch 3, 3 dc in same sp, work Block, slip st in ch-3 sp of last Block: 2 Blocks.

Row 5: Turn; slip st in first 3 dc and in first ch-3 sp, ch 3, 3 dc in same sp, slip st in ch-3 sp of last Block: 1 Block.

SECOND TRIANGLE

Row 1: Slip st across side of Triangle just made to next Block of Foundation Round, slip st in next 3 dc and in next ch-3 sp; ch 3, 3 dc in same sp, work 4 Blocks, slip st in ch-3 sp of next Block: 5 Blocks.

Rows 2-5: Work Same as First Triangle.
Repeat Second Triangle 26 times **more**.
Finish off.

CORNER FLOWER (Make 4)

Row 1 (Right side): With Color B ch 5, 3 dc in fifth ch from hook.
Note: Place marker to mark last row as **right** side.

Row 2: Work Beginning Block, slip st around beginning ch of previous Block, ch 3, 3 dc in same sp: 2 Blocks.

Row 3: Work Beginning Block, slip st in ch-3 sp of first Block, ch 3, 3 dc in same sp, work Block, changing to Color C in last dc: 3 Blocks.

Row 4: Work Beginning Block, slip st in ch-3 sp of first Block, ch 3, 3 dc in same sp, work 2 Blocks: 4 Blocks.

Row 5: Work Beginning Block, slip st in ch-3 sp of first Block, ch 3, 3 dc in same sp; with Color D, work Block; with Color C, work 2 Blocks: 5 Blocks.

Row 6: Work Beginning Block, slip st in ch-3 sp of first Block, ch 3, 3 dc in same sp; with Color D, work 2 Blocks; with Color C, work 2 Blocks: 6 Blocks.

Row 7: Work Beginning Block, slip st in ch-3 sp of first Block, ch 3, 3 dc in same sp; with Color D, work 3 Blocks; with Color C, work 2 Blocks; finish off: 7 Blocks.

Row 8: With **wrong** side facing, skip first Block and join Color D with slip st in ch-3 sp of next Block; ch 3, 3 dc in same sp, work 3 Blocks, slip st in ch-3 sp of next Block; finish off: 4 Blocks.

Row 9: With **right** side facing, skip first Block and join Color C with slip st in ch-3 sp of next Block; ch 3, 3 dc in same sp, slip st in ch-3 sp of next Block; finish off.

FLOWER (Make 28)

Rows 1-6: Work Same as Corner Flower: 6 Blocks.

Row 7: Work Beginning Block, slip st in ch-3 sp of first Block, ch 3, 3 dc in same sp; with Color D, work 3 Blocks; with Color C, work Block, slip st in ch-3 sp of last Block; finish off.

Row 8: With **wrong** side facing, join Color D with slip st in ch-3 sp of first Block; ch 3, 3 dc in same sp, work 3 Blocks, slip st in ch-3 sp of next Block; finish off: 4 Blocks.

Row 9: With **right** side facing, skip first Block and join Color C with slip st in ch-3 sp of next Block; ch 3, 3 dc in same sp, slip st in ch-3 sp of next Block; finish off.

JOINING

Whipstitch a Flower between first two Triangles on top right corner of any side, being careful to match rows.
Note: The last Block on the right will be joined later to the Corner Piece.
Whipstitch the next Flower between the next two Triangles, joining the last Block on the right to the previous Flower.

Repeat along the side.
Join Flowers in same manner to remaining three sides.

CORNER PIECE (Make 4)

With Flower facing and beginning at Row 1, whipstitch one Flower and one Corner Flower together. Whipstitch bottom of each Corner Piece across each corner of Afghan.

FOURTH OF JULY FANFARE

Summer wouldn't be complete without the flag-waving festivities of the Fourth of July. Patriotic colors let this bold afghan capture some of the fun of the season.

Finished Size: Approximately 43" x 55"

MATERIALS

Worsted Weight Yarn, approximately:
Color A (Blue) - 14½ ounces,
(410 grams, 955 yards)
Color B (Red) - 15 ounces, (430 grams, 985 yards)
Color C (Ecru) - 13½ ounces,
(380 grams, 885 yards)
Crochet hook, size J (6.00 mm) **or** size needed for gauge

GAUGE: In pattern, 12 sts and 10 rows = 4"

STRIPE SEQUENCE

3 Rows Color A, 4 rows Color B, 4 rows Color C, ★ 4 rows Color A, 4 rows Color B, 4 rows Color C; repeat from ★ 9 times **more**, 3 rows Color A.

With Color A, ch 127 **loosely.**
Row 1: Hdc in third ch from hook and in each ch across: 125 hdc.
Rows 2 and 3: Ch 2, turn; hdc in first hdc and in each hdc across, changing to Color B in last hdc of Row 3 *(Fig. 21, page 141)*.
Note: Work Front Post treble crochet *(abbreviated FPtr)* as follows: YO twice, insert hook from **front** to **back** around post of st indicated *(Fig. 13d, page 138)*, YO and pull up a loop, (YO and draw through 2 loops on hook) 3 times.
Row 4 (Right side): Ch 2, turn; hdc in first hdc, (work FPtr around hdc **below** next hdc) 3 times, skip 3 sts behind FPtr **(now and throughout)**, ★ hdc in next 3 hdc, (work FPtr around hdc **below** next hdc) 3 times; repeat from ★ across to last hdc, hdc in last hdc.

Row 5: Ch 2, turn; hdc in first st and in each st across.
Row 6: Ch 2, turn; hdc in first hdc, work FPtr around next 3 FPtr, ★ hdc in next 3 hdc, work FPtr around next 3 FPtr; repeat from ★ across to last hdc, hdc in last hdc.
Row 7: Ch 2, turn; hdc in first st and in each st across, changing to next color in last hdc.
Row 8: Ch 2, turn; hdc in first 4 hdc, (work FPtr around hdc **below** next hdc) 3 times, ★ hdc in next 3 hdc, (work FPtr around hdc **below** next hdc) 3 times; repeat from ★ across to last 4 hdc, hdc in last 4 hdc.
Row 9: Ch 2, turn; hdc in first st and in each st across.
Row 10: Ch 2, turn; hdc in first 4 hdc, work FPtr around next 3 FPtr, ★ hdc in next 3 hdc, work FPtr around next 3 FPtr; repeat from ★ across to last 4 hdc, hdc in last 4 hdc.
Row 11: Ch 2, turn; hdc in first st and in each st across, changing to next color in last hdc.
Rows 12-134: Repeat Rows 4-11, 15 times; then repeat Rows 4-6 once **more**, changing to Color B in last hdc of last row.

EDGING

Rnd 1: Ch 1, do **not** turn; working in end of rows, work 162 sc evenly spaced across; working in free loops of beginning ch *(Fig. 19b, page 140)*, 3 sc in first ch (corner), sc in each ch across to last ch, 3 sc in last ch (corner); working in end of rows, work 162 sc evenly spaced across; working across last row, 3 sc in first st (corner), sc in each st across to last st, 3 sc in last st (corner); join with slip st to first sc: 582 sc.
Rnd 2: Ch 2, do **not** turn; working from **left** to **right**, work reverse hdc in next sc *(Figs. 15a-d, page 138)* and in each sc around; join with slip st to base of beginning ch-2, finish off.

BUBBLES FOR BABY

Bordered with a lovely shell edging trimmed with ribbon,
this dainty wrap and matching pillow for baby are
brimming with big, soft bubbles!

MATERIALS

Worsted Weight Yarn, approximately:
- **Afghan:** 27 ounces, (770 grams, 1,775 yards)
- **Pillow:** 9 ounces, (260 grams, 595 yards)

Crochet hook, size G (4.00 mm) **or** size needed for gauge

¼" Ribbon:
- **Afghan** - 5 yards
- **Pillow** - 2 yards

Polyester stuffing

GAUGE: In pattern, 2 Bubbles = 3", 7 rows = 4"

PATTERN STITCHES

BEGINNING BUBBLE
★ YO, insert hook in stitch indicated, YO and pull up a loop, YO and draw through 1 loop on hook, (YO and draw through 2 loops on hook) twice; repeat from ★ once **more**.

BUBBLE
★ YO, insert hook in stitch indicated, YO and pull up a loop, YO and draw through 1 loop on hook, (YO and draw through 2 loops on hook) twice; repeat from ★ 4 times **more**.

AFGHAN

Finished Size: Approximately 41" x 41"

Ch 157 **loosely**.

Row 1: Work beginning Bubble in fourth ch from hook, skip next 2 chs, sc in next ch, ★ skip next 2 chs, work Bubble in next ch, skip next 2 chs, sc in next ch; repeat from ★ across: 26 Bubbles.

Note: Work in Back Loops Only throughout *(Fig. 18, page 140)*.

Row 2: Ch 3, turn; work beginning Bubble in same st, (sc in center st of next Bubble, work Bubble in next sc) across, skip next 2 sts, sc in top of beginning ch.

Repeat Row 2 until afghan measures approximately 38½".

EDGING

Rnd 1: Ch 1, turn; sc in Back Loop Only of each st across to last st, 3 sc in last st; work 153 sc evenly spaced across end of rows to last row, 3 sc in last row; working in free loops of beginning ch *(Fig. 19b, page 140)*, sc in each ch across to last ch, 3 sc in last ch; work 153 sc evenly spaced across end of rows to last row, 3 sc in last row; join with slip st to first sc: 624 sc.

Rnd 2 (Eyelet rnd): Working in **both** loops, slip st in next sc, ch 4, skip next 2 sc, (hdc in next sc, ch 2, skip next 2 sc) around; join with slip st to second ch of beginning ch-4: 208 ch-2 sps.

Rnd 3: Ch 1, sc in same st, 5 dc in next hdc, (sc in next hdc, 5 dc in next hdc) around; join with slip st to first sc, finish off.

Weave ribbon through Eyelet rnd and tie in a bow at corner.

PILLOW

Finished Size: Approximately 11" x 15½"

FRONT

Ch 67 **loosely**.

Work same as afghan until Front measures approximately 11": 11 Bubbles.

Finish off.

BACK

Work same as Front; do **not** finish off.

EDGING

Rnd 1: Ch 1, turn; with both pieces together and working in Back Loops Only, sc in each st across to last st, 3 sc in last st; work 33 sc evenly spaced across end of rows to last row, 3 sc in last row; working in free loops of beginning ch *(Fig. 19b, page 140)*, sc in each ch across to last ch, 3 sc in last ch; add stuffing; work 33 sc evenly spaced across end of rows to last row, 3 sc in last row; join with slip st to first sc: 204 sc.

Rnds 2 and 3: Work same as afghan: 68 ch-2 sps.

Weave ribbon through Eyelet rnd and tie in a bow at center bottom.

PICKET FENCES

This easy-to-crochet afghan is a variation of the popular mile-a-minute pattern. Our color scheme enhances the vision it creates of white picket fences and freshly mown lawns.

Finished Size: Approximately 52" x 70"

MATERIALS
Worsted Weight Yarn, approximately:
MC (Ecru) - 34 ounces, (970 grams, 2,235 yards)
CC (Green) - 17 ounces, (480 grams, 1,115 yards)
Crochet hook, size J (6.00 mm) **or** size needed for gauge
Yarn needle

GAUGE: 16 dc and 8 rows = 4"
One Strip = 4" wide

STRIP (Make 13)
CENTER SHELLS
With MC, ch 250 **loosely**.
Rnd 1 (Right side): 4 Dc in fourth ch from hook, tie a scrap piece of yarn around last dc made to mark Rnd 2 placement and **right** side, dc in next ch and in each ch across to last ch, 5 dc in last ch; working in free loops of beginning ch *(Fig. 19b, page 140)*, dc in next 245 chs; join with slip st to top of beginning ch, finish off: 500 sts.
Rnd 2: With **right** side facing, join CC with slip st in marked dc; ch 3 **(counts as first dc, now and throughout)**, 4 dc in same st, † ★ skip next 2 dc, work FPdc around next dc *(Fig. 13c, page 137)*, skip dc behind FPdc **and** next 2 dc, 5 dc in next dc; repeat from ★ 40 times **more**, skip next dc, 2 tr in next dc (center dc of 5-dc group), work FPtr around post of same dc *(Fig. 13d, page 138)*, 2 tr in same dc, skip next dc †, 5 dc in next dc, repeat from † to † once; join with slip st to first dc, finish off: 42 5-dc groups **each** side.

EDGING
FIRST SIDE
Row 1: With **right** side facing, join MC with slip st in BLO of center dc of first 5-dc group *(Fig. 18, page 140)*; ch 3, dc in BLO of next 2 dc, work FPtr around next FPdc, skip st behind FPtr, ★ dc in BLO of next 5 dc, work FPtr around next FPdc, skip st behind FPtr; repeat from ★ 39 times **more**, dc in BLO of next 3 dc, leave remaining sts unworked; finish off: 247 sts.
Row 2: With **right** side facing and working in both loops, join MC with slip st in first dc; ch 1, sc in same st and in next 2 dc, work FPhdc around next FPtr *(Fig. 13b, page 137)*, skip st behind FPhdc, ★ sc in next 5 dc, work FPhdc around next FPtr, skip st behind FPhdc; repeat from ★ across to last 3 dc, sc in last 3 dc; finish off.

SECOND SIDE
Work same as First Side.

JOINING
Using MC, whipstitch Strips together working through inside loops *(Fig. 23b, page 141)*.
Join remaining Strips in same manner, always working from the same direction.

BORDER
With **right** side of long edge facing, join CC with slip st in first sc; ch 1, 2 sc in same st, † sc in each st across to last sc, 2 sc in last sc, skip first sc row, 2 sc in end of next dc row; working in BLO, sc in next 2 dc, 2 sc in each of next 5 sts, sc in next 2 dc, 2 sc in end of next dc row, skip next sc row, ★ sc in joining, skip next sc row, 2 sc in end of next dc row; working in BLO, sc in next 2 dc, 2 sc in each of next 5 sts, sc in next 2 dc, 2 sc in end of next dc row, skip next sc row; repeat from ★ across to corner †, 2 sc in first sc, repeat from † to † once; join with slip st to first sc, finish off.

IRRESISTIBLE RIPPLES

*Cluster stitches create a lacy effect that gives this
ripple afghan irresistible charm.*

Finished Size: Approximately 52" x 70"

MATERIALS
Worsted Weight Yarn, approximately:
Color A (Dark Blue) - 8 ounces,
  (230 grams, 525 yards)
Color B (Medium Blue) - 13 ounces,
  (370 grams, 855 yards)
Color C (Light Blue) - 13 ounces,
  (370 grams, 855 yards)
Color D (Ecru) - 7 ounces, (200 grams, 460 yards)
Crochet hook, size I (5.50 mm) **or** size needed for
gauge

GAUGE: In pattern, 2 repeats = 8½"
  8 rows = 4½"
  Gauge Swatch (8½" x 4½"):
  Ch 51 **loosely**.
  Work same as Afghan for 8 rows.

PATTERN STITCHES
CLUSTER (worked across 3 chs)
Pull up a loop in next 3 chs, YO and draw through all
4 loops on hook.
DECREASE
Pull up a loop in next 6 chs, YO and draw through all
7 loops on hook.

COLOR SEQUENCE
Two rows **each**: Color A, ★ Color B, Color C, Color D,
Color C, Color B, Color A; repeat from ★ 9 times
more.

With Color A, ch 291 **loosely**.
Row 1: Insert hook in third ch from hook, YO and pull
up a loop, pull up a loop in next 2 chs, YO and draw
through all 4 loops on hook, (ch 3, work Cluster) 3
times, ch 6, (work Cluster, ch 3) 3 times, ★ decrease,
(ch 3, work Cluster) 3 times, ch 6, (work Cluster, ch 3)
3 times; repeat from ★ across to last 4 chs, work
Cluster, hdc in last ch.

Note: Work in Back Loop Only throughout *(Fig. 18,
page 140)*.
Row 2 (Right side): Ch 2, turn; skip first Cluster, work
Cluster, (ch 3, skip next Cluster, work Cluster) 3 times,
ch 6, (work Cluster, ch 3, skip next Cluster) 3 times,
★ decrease, (ch 3, skip next Cluster, work Cluster) 3
times, ch 6, (work Cluster, ch 3, skip next Cluster) 3
times; repeat from ★ across to last ch-3 sp, work
Cluster, skip next Cluster, hdc in top of beginning ch;
finish off.
Note: Loop a short piece of yarn around any stitch to
mark last row as **right** side.
Row 3: With **wrong** side facing, join next color with
slip st in first hdc; ch 2, skip first Cluster, work Cluster,
(ch 3, skip next Cluster, work Cluster) 3 times, ch 6,
(work Cluster, ch 3, skip next Cluster) 3 times,
★ decrease, (ch 3, skip next Cluster, work Cluster) 3
times, ch 6, (work Cluster, ch 3, skip next Cluster) 3
times; repeat from ★ across to last ch-3 sp, work
Cluster, skip next Cluster, hdc in top of beginning ch;
do **not** finish off.
Rows 4-122: Repeat Rows 2 and 3, 59 times; then
repeat Row 2 once **more**; at end of Row 122 do **not**
finish off.

EDGING

Ch 1, do **not** turn; working in end of rows, slip st in
first row, (ch 1, slip st in next row) across to last row,
ch 1, (slip st, ch 3, slip st) in last row; working in sp
between Clusters, (ch 3, slip st in next sp) 3 times,
(ch 1, slip st in next sp) twice, ch 3, (slip st in next sp,
ch 3) twice, † (slip st, ch 3, slip st) in center of next
decrease, (ch 3, slip st in next sp) 3 times, (ch 1, slip st
in next sp) twice, ch 3, (slip st in next sp, ch 3) twice †,
repeat from † to † 10 times **more**; working in end of
rows, (slip st, ch 3, slip st) in first row, (ch 1, slip st in
next row) across, ch 3; slip st in first ch-3 sp, ch 3,
(slip st in next ch-3 sp, ch 3) twice, (slip st, ch 3, slip st)
in next ch-6 sp, ★ ch 3, (slip st in next ch-3 sp, ch 3) 6
times, (slip st, ch 3, slip st) in next ch-6 sp; repeat from
★ 10 times **more**, ch 3, (slip st in next ch-3 sp, ch 3) 3
times; join with slip st to first st, finish off.

DELIGHTFUL DAISIES

*Emblems of fidelity and innocence, daisies are a favorite flower
during the summer months. The lovely openwork flowers
lend a gentle, breezy touch to this simple afghan.*

Finished Size: Approximately 56″ x 61″

MATERIALS
Worsted Weight Yarn, approximately:
   47 ounces, (1,340 grams, 2,990 yards)
Crochet hook, size G (4.00 mm) **or** size needed for
   gauge

GAUGE: 16 dc and 8 rows = 4″

Ch 224 **loosely**.
Row 1: Dc in eighth ch from hook, ★ ch 2, skip next
2 chs, dc in next ch; repeat from ★ across: 73 ch-2 sps.
Row 2 (Right side)**:** Ch 5 **(counts as first dc plus ch 2,
now and throughout)**, turn; dc in next dc, ★ 2 dc in next
ch-2 sp, dc in next dc; repeat from ★ across to last sp,
ch 2, skip next 2 chs, dc in next ch: 216 dc.
Row 3: Ch 5, turn; dc in next 5 dc, ch 3, skip next dc,
tr in next dc, ch 1, skip next 2 dc, tr in next dc, ch 3,
★ skip next dc, dc in next 16 dc, ch 3, skip next dc, tr in
next dc, ch 1, skip next 2 dc, tr in next dc, ch 3; repeat
from ★ 8 times **more**, skip next dc, dc in next 5 dc, ch 2,
dc in last dc.
Row 4: Ch 5, turn; dc in next 3 dc, ch 3, sc in next
ch-3 sp, sc in next ch-1 sp, sc in next ch-3 sp, ch 3,
★ skip next 2 dc, dc in next 12 dc, ch 3, sc in next
ch-3 sp, sc in next ch-1 sp, sc in next ch-3 sp, ch 3;
repeat from ★ 8 times **more**, skip next 2 dc, dc in next
3 dc, ch 2, dc in last dc.
Row 5: Ch 5, turn; dc in next 3 dc, ch 3, sc in next 3 sc,
ch 3, ★ dc in next 12 dc, ch 3, sc in next 3 sc, ch 3; repeat
from ★ 8 times **more**, dc in next 3 dc, ch 2, dc in last dc.
Row 6: Ch 5, turn; dc in next 3 dc, 2 dc in next ch-3 sp,
ch 1, skip next sc, (tr, ch 2, tr) in next sc, ch 1, 2 dc in
next ch-3 sp, ★ dc in next 12 dc, 2 dc in next ch-3 sp,
ch 1, skip next sc, (tr, ch 2, tr) in next sc, ch 1, 2 dc in
next ch-3 sp; repeat from ★ 8 times **more**, dc in next
3 dc, ch 2, dc in last dc.
Row 7: Ch 5, turn; dc in next 5 dc, dc in next ch-1 sp,
dc in next tr, 2 dc in next ch-2 sp, dc in next tr, dc in
next ch-1 sp, dc in next 5 dc, ★ ch 3, skip next dc, tr in
next dc, ch 1, skip next 2 dc, tr in next dc, ch 3, skip
next dc, dc in next 5 dc, dc in next ch-1 sp, dc in next tr,
2 dc in next ch-2 sp, dc in next tr, dc in next ch-1 sp,
dc in next 5 dc; repeat from ★ 8 times **more**, ch 2, dc in
last dc.

Row 8: Ch 5, turn; dc in next 14 dc, ch 3, sc in next
ch-3 sp, sc in next ch-1 sp, sc in next ch-3 sp, ch 3, skip
next 2 dc, ★ dc in next 12 dc, ch 3, sc in next ch-3 sp, sc
in next ch-1 sp, sc in next ch-3 sp, ch 3, skip next 2 dc;
repeat from ★ 7 times **more**, dc in next 14 dc, ch 2, dc in
last dc.
Row 9: Ch 5, turn; dc in next 14 dc, ch 3, sc in next 3 sc,
ch 3, ★ dc in next 12 dc, ch 3, sc in next 3 sc, ch 3; repeat
from ★ 7 times **more**, dc in next 14 dc, ch 2, dc in last
dc.
Row 10: Ch 5, turn; dc in next 14 dc, 2 dc in next
ch-3 sp, ch 1, skip next sc, (tr, ch 2, tr) in next sc, ch 1,
2 dc in next ch-3 sp, ★ dc in next 12 dc, 2 dc in next
ch-3 sp, ch 1, skip next sc, (tr, ch 2, tr) in next sc, ch 1,
2 dc in next ch-3 sp; repeat from ★ 7 times **more**, dc in
next 14 dc, ch 2, dc in last dc.
Row 11: Ch 5, turn; dc in next 5 dc, ch 3, skip next dc,
tr in next dc, ch 1, skip next 2 dc, tr in next dc, ch 3,
skip next dc, dc in next 5 dc, ★ dc in next ch-1 sp, dc in
next tr, 2 dc in next ch-2 sp, dc in next tr, dc in next
ch-1 sp, dc in next 5 dc, ch 3, skip next dc, tr in next dc,
ch 1, skip next 2 dc, tr in next dc, ch 3, skip next dc,
dc in next 5 dc; repeat from ★ 8 times **more**, ch 2, dc in
last dc.
Rows 12-115: Repeat Rows 4-11, 13 times.
Rows 116-118: Repeat Rows 4-6.
Row 119: Ch 5, turn; dc in next 5 dc, dc in next ch-1 sp,
dc in next tr, 2 dc in next ch-2 sp, dc in next tr, dc in
next ch-1 sp, ★ dc in next 16 dc, dc in next ch-1 sp, dc in
next tr, 2 dc in next ch-2 sp, dc in next tr, dc in next
ch-1 sp; repeat from ★ 8 times **more**, dc in next 5 dc,
ch 2, dc in last dc: 216 dc.
Row 120: Ch 5, turn; dc in next dc, ★ ch 2, skip next
2 dc, dc in next dc; repeat from ★ across to last sp, ch 2,
dc in last dc; do **not** finish off: 73 ch-2 sps.

EDGING

Ch 1, do **not** turn; working in end of rows, ch 1, 3 sc in
corner sp, 2 sc in next sp and in each sp across to next
corner sp, ★ 5 sc in corner sp, 2 sc in next sp and in
each sp across to next corner sp; repeat from ★ 2 times
more, 2 sc in first corner sp; join with slip st to first sc,
finish off.

Add fringe *(Figs. 25a & b, page 142)*.

ELEGANT DAISY CHAIN

*Fashioned all in one color, this lacy throw features a variety
of stitches to let you show off your crocheting skills.
Its rich texture adds elegance to any setting.*

Finished Size: Approximately 48" x 70"

MATERIALS
Worsted Weight Yarn, approximately:
    52 ounces, (1,480 grams, 3,420 yards)
Crochet hook, size I (5.50 mm) **or** size needed for
    gauge
Yarn needle

GAUGE: In pattern, 4 Lace Sts and 1 strip = 4"
            1 Daisy = 2½"

PATTERN STITCHES
SHELL
(Tr, ch 1) 5 times in space indicated.
LACE STITCH
Ch 3, 2 dc in third ch from hook.

STRIP (Make 12)
FIRST SIDE

Foundation Chain: Ch 7 **loosely**, dc in third ch from
hook (ring), (ch 10 **loosely**, dc in third ch from hook)
27 times, ch 5 **loosely**: 28 rings.
Row 1 (Right side): Sc in second ch from hook, ★ ch 1,
work Shell in next ring, skip next 3 chs, sc in next ch;
repeat from ★ across: 28 Shells.
Note: Loop a short piece of yarn around first stitch to
mark last row as **right** side and top.
Row 2: Ch 1, turn; slip st in first sc, (ch 2, skip next
ch-1 sp, slip st in next st) across: 168 ch-2 sps.
Note: Work decrease as follows: ★ YO twice, insert
hook in **next** ch-1 sp, YO and pull up a loop, (YO and
draw through 2 loops on hook) twice; repeat from ★
once **more**, YO and draw through all 3 loops on hook.
Row 3: Ch 3, turn; working **behind** ch-2 and in
ch-1 sps on Row 1, tr in next ch-1 sp, ch 1, dc in next
ch-1 sp, ch 1, (sc in next ch-1 sp, ch 1) twice, dc in next
ch-1 sp, ch 1, ★ decrease, ch 1, dc in next ch-1 sp, ch 1,
(sc in next ch-1 sp, ch 1) twice, dc in next ch-1 sp, ch 1;
repeat from ★ across to last ch-1 sp, YO twice, insert
hook in last ch-1 sp, YO and pull up a loop, (YO and
draw through 2 loops on hook) twice, YO twice,
insert hook in last slip st, YO and pull up a loop,
(YO and draw through 2 loops on hook) twice, YO
and draw through all 3 loops on hook: 140 ch-1 sps.

Row 4: Ch 1, turn; sc in first st, (work Lace St, skip
next 2 ch-1 sps, sc in next st) across to last 2 ch-1 sps,
work Lace St, skip last 2 ch-1 sps, sc in top of
turning ch: 70 Lace Sts.
Row 5: Ch 4, turn; working **behind** Lace St, skip next
ch-1 sp on Row 3, tr in next st on Row 3, ch 1, dc in
next sc on Row 4, ★ ch 1, working **behind** Lace St,
skip next ch-1 sp on Row 3, tr in next st on Row 3, ch 1,
dc in next sc on Row 4; repeat from ★ across; finish off.

SECOND SIDE
Row 1: With **right** side facing and working in free
loops of Foundation Chain *(Fig. 19b, page 140)*, join
yarn with slip st in first ch; ch 1, sc in same st, ★ ch 1,
work Shell in next ring, skip next 3 chs, sc in next ch;
repeat from ★ across: 28 Shells.
Row 2: Ch 1, turn; slip st in first sc, ch 2, (slip st in next
tr, ch 2) 5 times, ★ slip st in next slip st on Row 2 of
First Side (between Shells), ch 2, skip next sc, (slip st
in next tr, ch 2) 5 times; repeat from ★ across to last sc,
slip st in last sc.
Rows 3-5: Work same as Rows 3-5 of First Side.

JOINING
Whipstitch strips together, with marked edges at top
and working through both loops *(Fig. 23a, page 141)*.

EDGING
With **right** side facing, join yarn with slip st in first row
of top right corner; ch 2, slip st in same sp, † working
in end of rows, ★ ch 2, (skip next row, slip st in next
row, ch 2) 5 times, skip joining, slip st in next row;
repeat from ★ across to last Strip, ch 2, (skip next row,
slip st in next row, ch 2) 4 times, skip next row, (slip st,
ch 2, slip st) in next corner, ch 1, (slip st in next ch-1 sp,
ch 1) across to next corner †, (slip st, ch 2, slip st) in
corner, repeat from † to † once; join with slip st to
first st, finish off.

Add fringe *(Figs. 25a & b, page 142)*.

RAINBOW DIAMONDS

*Want to shower baby with love? Then you'll want to crochet
this darling afghan! It features a rainbow of miniature
granny squares that you join as you go.*

Finished Size: Approximately 40″ x 40″

MATERIALS

Sport Weight Yarn, approximately:
MC (White) - 7 ounces, (200 grams, 700 yards)
Lavender (L) - 2 ounces, (60 grams, 200 yards)
Blue (B) - 2 ounces, (60 grams, 200 yards)
Green (G) - 2 ounces, (60 grams, 200 yards)
Pink (P) - 2 ounces, (60 grams, 200 yards)
Orange or Peach (O) - 2 ounces,
    (60 grams, 200 yards)
Yellow (Y) - 2 ounces, (60 grams, 200 yards)
Crochet hook, size D (3.25 mm) **or** size needed for
gauge

GAUGE: One Square = 2″

Beginning at center of Placement Chart, page 60, make
Squares using color indicated.

FIRST SQUARE

Ch 4, join with slip st to form a ring.
Rnd 1 (Right side): Ch 2, (YO, insert hook in ring,
YO and pull up a loop, YO and draw through 2 loops
on hook) twice, YO and draw through all 3 loops on
hook, ch 4, ★ (YO, insert hook in ring, YO and pull up
a loop, YO and draw through 2 loops on hook) 3
times, YO and draw through all 4 loops on hook, ch 4;
repeat from ★ 2 times **more**; join with slip st to top of
first st: 4 ch-4 sps.
Note: Loop a short piece of yarn around any stitch to
mark last round as **right** side.
Rnd 2: Slip st in first ch-4 sp, ch 3, (2 dc, ch 2, 3 dc) in
same sp, ch 1, ★ (3 dc, ch 2, 3 dc) in next ch-4 sp, ch 1;
repeat from ★ around; join with slip st to top of
beginning ch-3, finish off: 8 sps.

ADDITIONAL SQUARES

Ch 4, join with slip st to form a ring.
Rnd 1: Work same as First Square.
Rnd 2: Work One or Two Side Joining.

ONE SIDE JOINING

Slip st in first ch-4 sp, ch 3, 2 dc in same sp, ch 1,
holding Squares with **wrong** sides together, slip st in
corner ch-2 sp on **previous Square**, ch 1, 3 dc in same
ch-4 sp on **new Square**, ch 1, slip st in next ch-1 sp on
previous Square *(Fig. 22, page 141)*, 3 dc in next
ch-4 sp on **new Square**, ch 1, slip st in next ch-2 sp on
previous Square, ch 1, 3 dc in same ch-4 sp on
new Square, ch 1, ★ (3 dc, ch 2, 3 dc) in next ch-4 sp,
ch 1; repeat from ★ around; join with slip st to top of
beginning ch-3, finish off.

TWO SIDE JOINING

Slip st in first ch-4 sp, ch 3, 2 dc in same sp, ch 1,
holding Squares with **wrong** sides together, ★ slip st in
corner ch-2 sp on **previous Square**, ch 1, 3 dc in same
ch-4 sp on **new Square**, ch 1, slip st in next ch-1 sp on
previous Square, 3 dc in next ch-4 sp on **new Square**,
ch 1, slip st in next ch-2 sp on **previous Square**, ch 1;
repeat from ★ once **more**, 3 dc in same ch-4 sp on **new
Square**, ch 1, (3 dc, ch 2, 3 dc) in next ch-4 sp, ch 1; join
with slip st to top of beginning ch-3, finish off.

EDGING

Rnd 1: With **right** side facing, join MC with slip st in any corner ch-2 sp; ch 1, 3 sc in same sp, sc in each dc and in each ch-sp around, working 3 sc in each corner ch-2 sp; join with slip st to first sc: 688 sc.

Rnd 2: Ch 3, 3 dc in next sc, dc in each sc around, working 3 dc in each corner sc; join with slip st to top of beginning ch-3: 696 sts.

Rnd 3: Ch 1, sc in same st, skip next dc, ★ † 7 dc in next dc, skip next dc, (sc in next dc, skip next dc, 5 dc in next dc, skip next 2 dc) across to within 2 dc of next corner dc †, sc in next dc, skip next dc; repeat from ★ 2 times **more**, then repeat from † to † once; join with slip st to first sc, finish off.

PLACEMENT CHART

	L	B		G	P		O	Y			Y	O		P	G			B	L	
L	B		G	P		O	Y			L		Y	O		P	G			B	L	
B		G	P		O	Y			L	B	L		Y	O		P	G			B	
	G	P		O	Y			L	B			B	L		Y	O		P	G		
G	P		O	Y			L	B		G		B	L		Y	O		P	G		
P		O	Y			L	B		G	P	G		B	L		Y	O		P		
	O	Y			L	B		G	P		P	G		B	L		Y	O			
O	Y			L	B		G	P		O		P	G		B	L		Y	O		
Y			L	B		G	P		O	Y	O		P	G		B	L		Y		
		L	B		G	P		O	Y		Y	O		P	G			B	L		
Y			L	B		G	P		O	Y	O		P	G		B	L		Y		
O	Y			L	B		G	P		O		P	G		B	L		Y	O		
	O	Y			L	B		G	P		P	G		B	L		Y	O			
P		O	Y			L	B		G	P	G		B	L		Y	O		P		
G	P		O	Y			L	B		G		B	L		Y	O		P	G		
	G	P		O	Y			L	B			B	L		Y	O		P	G		
B		G	P		O	Y			L	B	L		Y	O		P	G			B	
L	B		G	P		O	Y			L		Y	O		P	G			B	L	
	L	B		G	P		O	Y			Y	O		P	G			B	L		

HERITAGE AFGHAN

This beautiful crocheted afghan was inspired by a popular old star quilt pattern. Fashioned in soft country colors, it's a lovely way to combine the ease of crochet with the charm of quilts.

Finished Size: Approximately 46″ x 67″

MATERIALS

Worsted Weight Yarn, approximately:
MC (Blue) - 32 ounces, (910 grams, 2,160 yards)
CC (White) - 25 ounces, (710 grams, 1,680 yards)
Crochet hook, size G (4.00 mm) **or** size needed for gauge

GAUGE: 16 sc and 16 rows = 4″

Note: Entire Afghan is worked in one piece.

With MC, ch 174 **loosely**.
Row 1: Sc in second ch from hook and in each ch across: 173 sc.
Row 2 (Right side): Ch 1, turn; sc in each sc across.
Note #1: Loop a short piece of yarn around any stitch to mark last row as **right** side.

Note #2: When changing colors *(Fig. 21, page 141)*, work over color not being used, holding it with normal tension.

Note #3: On **right** side rows, work Chart from right to left; on **wrong** side rows, work from left to right.

Row 3: Begin following Chart as follows: Ch 1, turn; sc in first 2 sc (edge), ★ with CC sc in next sc, with MC sc in next 2 sc, with CC sc in next 11 sc, with MC sc in next 4 sc, with CC sc in next 2 sc, with MC sc in next 3 sc, with CC sc in next 2 sc, with MC sc in next 4 sc, with CC sc in next 11 sc, with MC sc in next 2 sc; repeat from ★ 3 times **more**, with CC sc in next sc, with MC sc in last 2 sc (edge).

Continue in pattern, following Chart through Row 44. Repeat Rows 3-44, 5 times; then repeat Row 3 once **more**.

Next 2 Rows: With MC ch 1, turn; sc in each sc across. Finish off.

EDGING

Rnd 1: With **right** side facing, join CC with slip st in any sc; ch 1, sc evenly around, working 3 sc in each corner; join with slip st to first sc.

Rnds 2-5: Ch 1, turn; sc in each sc around, working 3 sc in each corner; join with slip st to first sc. Finish off.

Rnd 6: With **right** side facing, join MC with slip st in any sc; ch 1, sc in each sc around, working 3 sc in each corner; join with slip st to first sc, finish off.

COLOR KEY

☐ - Blue

☐ - White

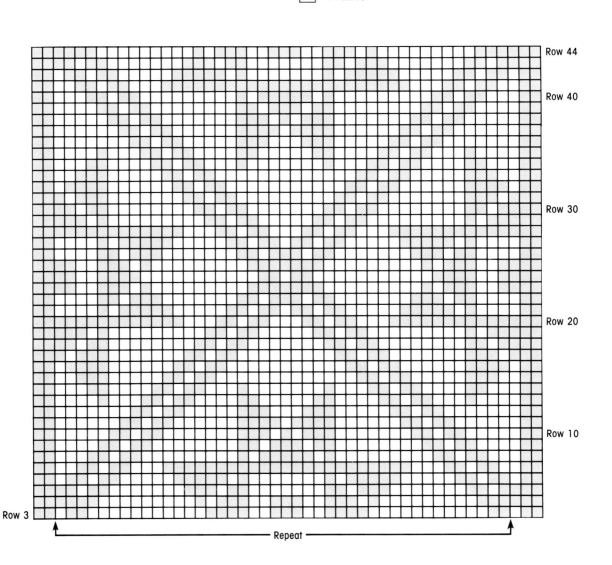

SUMMER FAVORITE

Symbolizing summer's favorite fruit, this delectable spread will preserve the flavor of warm weather picnics all through the year.

Finished Size: Approximately 47" x 60"

MATERIALS

Worsted Weight Yarn, approximately:
Main Color (Light Green) - 20 ounces,
(570 grams, 1,170 yards)
Color A (Green) - 11 ounces,
(310 grams, 645 yards)
Color B (Pink) - 9 ounces, (260 grams, 525 yards)
Color C (Light Pink) - 4 ounces,
(110 grams, 235 yards)
Crochet hook, size I (5.50 mm) **or** size needed for gauge

GAUGE: One Motif = 6½"

FIRST STRIP
FIRST MOTIF

With Color B ch 4, join with slip st to form a ring.
Rnd 1 (Right side): Ch 3 **(counts as first dc, now and throughout)**, 15 dc in ring; join with slip st to first dc: 16 dc.
Note: Loop a short piece of yarn around any stitch to mark last round as **right** side.
Rnd 2: Ch 3, dc in same st, 2 dc in next dc and in each dc around; join with slip st to first dc, finish off: 32 dc.
Rnd 3: With **right** side facing, join Color C with slip st in any dc; ch 2 **(counts as first hdc)**, hdc in next dc and in each dc around; join with slip st to first hdc, finish off.
Rnd 4: With **right** side facing, join Color A with slip st in any hdc; ch 3, dc in same st, 2 dc in next hdc and in each hdc around; join with slip st to first dc, finish off: 64 dc.
Rnd 5: With **right** side facing, join MC with slip st in any dc; ch 3, dc in same st, ch 2, 2 dc in next dc, skip next 2 dc, ★ 2 dc in next dc, ch 2, 2 dc in next dc, skip next 2 dc; repeat from ★ around; join with slip st to first dc, finish off: 16 ch-2 sps.

ADDITIONAL MOTIFS

Work same as First Motif through Rnd 4: 64 dc.
Rnd 5 (One Side Joining): With **right** side facing, join MC with slip st in any dc; ch 3, dc in same st, ch 1,

holding **previous Motif** adjacent with **right** side facing, sc in any ch-2 sp on **previous Motif**, ch 1, † 2 dc in next dc on **new Motif**, skip next 2 dc, 2 dc in next dc, ch 1, sc in next ch-2 sp on **previous Motif**, ch 1 †, repeat from † to † once **more**, 2 dc in next dc, skip next 2 dc, (2 dc in next dc, ch 2, 2 dc in next dc, skip next 2 dc) around; join with slip st to first dc, finish off.
To complete First Strip, work and join 7 **more** Motifs in the same manner, skipping 5 ch-2 sps on previous Motif when joining.

SECOND STRIP
FIRST MOTIF

Work same as First Motif of First Strip through Rnd 4: 64 dc.
Rnd 5 (One Side Joining): Work same as First Strip, skipping one ch-2 sp on First Motif of First Strip when joining.

ADDITIONAL MOTIFS

Work same as First Motif of First Strip through Rnd 4: 64 dc.
Rnd 5 (Two Side Joining): With **right** side facing, join MC with slip st in any dc; ch 3, dc in same st, ch 1, holding **previous Motif of First Strip** adjacent with right side facing, sc in second ch-2 sp on **previous Motif of First Strip** (to left of joining of Second and Third Motifs), ch 1, † 2 dc in next dc on **new Motif**, skip next 2 dc, 2 dc in next dc, ch 1, sc in next ch-2 sp on **previous Motif**, ch 1 †, repeat from † to † once **more**, 2 dc in next dc on new Motif, skip next 2 dc, 2 dc in next dc, ch 2, 2 dc in next dc, skip next 2 dc, 2 dc in next dc, ch 1, sc in second ch-2 sp on **previous Motif of Second Strip** (to left of joining of First Motifs), ch 1, repeat from † to † twice, 2 dc in next dc on **new Motif**, skip next 2 dc, (2 dc in next dc, ch 2, 2 dc in next dc, skip next 2 dc) around; join with slip st to first dc, finish off.
To complete Second Strip, work and join 7 **more** Motifs in the same manner.

REMAINING 5 STRIPS

Work in same manner as Second Strip.

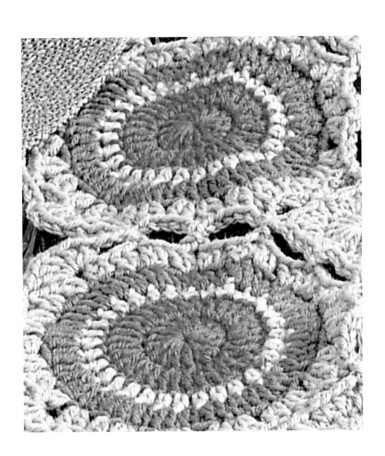

FILL-IN MOTIF

With MC ch 4, join with slip st to form a ring.

Rnd 1: Ch 3, 15 dc in ring; join with slip st to first dc: 16 dc.

Rnd 2 (Joining rnd): Ch 3, dc in same st, ch 1, holding Motifs with right side facing, slip st in sc of any Joining rnd, ★ † ch 1, 2 dc in next dc on **Fill-In Motif**, 2 hdc in next dc, ch 1, slip st in next ch-2 sp on **Motif**, ch 1, 2 hdc in next dc on **Fill-In Motif** †, 2 dc in next dc, ch 1, slip st in sc of next Joining rnd; repeat from ★ 2 times **more**, then repeat from † to † once; join with slip st to first dc, finish off.

Repeat for remaining 47 Fill-In Motifs.

EDGING

With **right** side facing, join MC with slip st in sc of any joining; ch 1, sc in same st, ★ † ch 2, dc in next ch-2 sp, (ch 1, dc) 4 times in same sp, ch 2, [sc in next ch-2 sp, ch 2, dc in next ch-2 sp, (ch 1, dc) 4 times in same sp, ch 2] across Motif to joining †, sc in sc of next joining; repeat from ★ around to last Motif, then repeat from † to † once; join with slip st to first sc, finish off.

AUTUMN

When fall is in the air, the earth is dressed in its most dazzling colors. Everywhere you look, vibrant gold, red, and orange leaves flutter in the season's crisp breezes and dance on the lawns. With a warm cover-up to ward off the chill, it's a lovely time to indulge in leisurely country drives and spirited gatherings at the stadium. This collection of earthy afghans — inspired by autumn's magnificent splendor— will wrap you in all the glory of this beautiful season.

SOFT STRIPES

This softly striped afghan combines the muted hues of fall
with the rich texture of picot stitches.

Finished Size: Approximately 45″ x 61″

MATERIALS

Bulky Weight Yarn, approximately:
 MC (Ecru) - 50 ounces, (1,420 grams, 2,290 yards)
 Color A (Tan) - 5 ounces,
  (140 grams, 230 yards)
 Color B (Apricot) - 5 ounces,
  (140 grams, 230 yards)
 Color C (Coral) - 5 ounces,
  (140 grams, 230 yards)
Crochet hook, size H (5.00 mm) **or** size needed for
 gauge

GAUGE: In pattern, 18 sts and 17 rows = 6″
 Gauge Swatch: (6″ x 6″)
 Ch 19 **loosely**.
 Work same as Afghan for 17 rows.
 Finish off.

STRIPE SEQUENCE

6 Rows MC **(Fig. 21, page 141)**, 2 rows Color A,
6 rows MC, 2 rows Color B, 6 rows MC,
✝ 2 rows Color C, 6 rows MC, 2 rows Color A,
6 rows MC, 2 rows Color B, 6 rows MC ✝, repeat
from ✝ to ✝ once **more**, 2 rows Color A, 6 rows MC,
★ 2 rows Color C, 6 rows MC, 2 rows Color B,
6 rows MC, 2 rows Color A, 6 rows MC; repeat
from ★ once **more**.

Note: Afghan is worked from side to side.

With MC, ch 184 **loosely**.
Row 1: Sc in second ch from hook and in each ch
across: 183 sc.
Row 2 (Right side): Ch 1, turn; sc in each sc across.
Note #1: Loop a short piece of yarn around any stitch
to mark last row as **right** side.
Note #2: Work Picot Shell as follows: (Dc, ch 3, slip st
in third ch from hook, dc) in next sc. Push Picot to
right side.
Row 3: Ch 3 **(counts as first dc, now and throughout)**,
turn; dc in next sc, (skip next sc, work Picot Shell)
across to last 3 sc, skip next sc, dc in last 2 sc:
89 Picot Shells.
Row 4: Ch 3, turn; dc in same st and in each dc across:
183 dc.
Rows 5-10: Ch 1, turn; sc in each st across.
Rows 11-126: Repeat Rows 3-10, 14 times; then repeat
Rows 3-6 once **more**.
Finish off.

Add fringe **(Figs. 25a & b, page 142)**.

HARVEST GOLD

*This lacy pineapple afghan captures all the golden
glory of the harvest season.*

Finished Size: Approximately 47″ x 64″

MATERIALS
Worsted Weight Brushed Acrylic Yarn,
approximately:
   32½ ounces, (930 grams, 2,510 yards)
Crochet hook, size I (5.50 mm) **or** size needed for
gauge

GAUGE: One Strip = 5½″ wide
   Gauge Swatch: (5½″ x 5½″)
   Work same as Strip for 8 rows.
   Finish off.

STRIP (Make 8)

Ch 8, join with slip st to form a ring.
Row 1 (Right side): Ch 3 **(counts as first dc, now and throughout)**, work (dc, ch 2, 2 dc, ch 1, 11 tr, ch 1, 2 dc, ch 2, 2 dc) in ring: 25 sts.
Note: Loop a short piece of yarn around any stitch to mark last row as **right** side.
Row 2: Ch 2, turn; (2 dc, ch 2, 2 dc) in first ch-2 sp, ch 1, skip next ch-1 sp, sc in next tr, (ch 3, skip next tr, sc in next tr) 5 times, ch 1, skip next ch-1 sp, (2 dc, ch 2, 2 dc) in last ch-2 sp: 5 ch-3 sps.
Row 3: Ch 2, place marker around ch-2 just worked, turn; (2 dc, ch 2, 2 dc) in first ch-2 sp, ch 2, skip next ch-1 sp, sc in next ch-3 sp, (ch 3, sc in next ch-3 sp) 4 times, ch 2, skip next ch-1 sp, (2 dc, ch 2, 2 dc) in last ch-2 sp: 4 ch-3 sps.
Row 4: Ch 2, place marker around ch-2 just worked, turn; (2 dc, ch 2, 2 dc) in first ch-2 sp, ch 2, skip next ch-2 sp, sc in next ch-3 sp, (ch 3, sc in next ch-3 sp) 3 times, ch 2, skip next ch-2 sp, (2 dc, ch 2, 2 dc) in last ch-2 sp: 3 ch-3 sps.
Row 5: Ch 2, turn; (2 dc, ch 2, 2 dc) in first ch-2 sp, ch 2, skip next ch-2 sp, sc in next ch-3 sp, (ch 3, sc in next ch-3 sp) twice, ch 2, skip next ch-2 sp, (2 dc, ch 2, 2 dc) in last ch-2 sp: 2 ch-3 sps.
Row 6: Ch 2, turn; (2 dc, ch 2, 2 dc) in first ch-2 sp, ch 3, skip next ch-2 sp, (sc in next ch-3 sp, ch 3) twice, skip next ch-2 sp, (2 dc, ch 2, 2 dc) in last ch-2 sp: 3 ch-3 sps.
Row 7: Ch 2, turn; (2 dc, ch 2, 2 dc) in first ch-2 sp, ch 3, skip next ch-3 sp, (dc, ch 2, dc) in next ch-3 sp, ch 3, skip next ch-3 sp, (2 dc, ch 2, 2 dc) in last ch-2 sp: 2 ch-3 sps.

Row 8: Ch 2, turn; (2 dc, ch 2, 2 dc) in first ch-2 sp, ch 1, skip next ch-3 sp, 11 tr in next ch-2 sp, ch 1, skip next ch-3 sp, (2 dc, ch 2, 2 dc) in last ch-2 sp.
Row 9: Ch 2, turn; (2 dc, ch 2, 2 dc) in first ch-2 sp, ch 1, skip next ch-1 sp, sc in next tr, (ch 3, skip next tr, sc in next tr) 5 times, ch 1, skip next ch-1 sp, (2 dc, ch 2, 2 dc) in last ch-2 sp: 5 ch-3 sps.
Row 10: Ch 2, turn; (2 dc, ch 2, 2 dc) in first ch-2 sp, ch 2, skip next ch-1 sp, sc in next ch-3 sp, (ch 3, sc in next ch-3 sp) 4 times, ch 2, skip next ch-1 sp, (2 dc, ch 2, 2 dc) in last ch-2 sp: 4 ch-3 sps.
Row 11: Ch 2, turn; (2 dc, ch 2, 2 dc) in first ch-2 sp, ch 2, skip next ch-2 sp, sc in next ch-3 sp, (ch 3, sc in next ch-3 sp) 3 times, ch 2, skip next ch-2 sp, (2 dc, ch 2, 2 dc) in last ch-2 sp: 3 ch-3 sps.
Rows 12-98: Repeat Rows 5-11, 12 times; then repeat Rows 5-7 once **more**.
Row 99: Ch 2, turn; (2 dc, ch 2, 2 dc) in first ch-2 sp, ch 3, skip next ch-3 sp, dc in next ch-2 sp, ch 3, skip next ch-3 sp, (2 dc, ch 2, 2 dc) in last ch-2 sp: 2 ch-3 sps.
Row 100: Ch 2, turn; (2 dc, ch 2, 2 dc) in first ch-2 sp, ch 2, skip next ch-3 sp, sc in next dc, ch 2, skip next ch-3 sp, (2 dc, ch 2, 2 dc) in last ch-2 sp.
Row 101: Ch 2, turn; slip st in first ch-2 sp, ch 2, skip next 2 ch-2 sps, slip st in last ch-2 sp; finish off.

EDGING

With **right** side of first Strip facing and working in end of rows, join yarn with slip st in marked sp on right edge; ch 1, sc in same sp, ★ ch 5, skip next row, sc in ch-2 sp on next row; repeat from ★ 45 times **more**; finish off.
Repeat for six more Strips, leaving one Strip unworked to be joined first.

JOINING

With **wrong** side of **new Strip** facing and working in end of rows, join yarn with slip st in marked sp on right edge; ch 1, sc in same sp, ch 2, having **previous Strip** adjacent with **wrong** side facing, slip st in first ch-5 sp on **previous Strip**, ch 2, skip next row on **new Strip**, sc in ch-2 sp on next row, ★ ch 2, slip st in next ch-5 sp on **previous Strip**, ch 2, skip next row on **new Strip**, sc in ch-2 sp on next row; repeat from ★ 44 times **more**; finish off.
Join remaining Strips in same manner.

TEXTURED BANDS

Worked from side to side in bands, this classic comforter offers a potpourri of pretty textures! A simple fringe adds an air of elegance.

Finished Size: Approximately 53″ x 69″

MATERIALS

Worsted Weight Yarn, approximately:
   57 ounces, (1,620 grams, 3,745 yards)
Crochet hooks, sizes G (4.00 mm) **and** I (5.50 mm)
   or sizes needed for gauge

GAUGE: In pattern, with larger size hook, 20 sts = 4″
   Gauge Swatch: (4¼″ x 4½″)
   Ch 22.
   Work same as Afghan for 21 rows.
   Finish off.

Note: Afghan is worked from side to side.

CLUSTER

★ YO, insert hook in st indicated, YO and pull up a loop, YO and draw 2 loops on hook; repeat from ★ once **more**, YO and draw through all 3 loops on hook *(Figs. 9a & b, page 135)*. Push Cluster to **right** side.

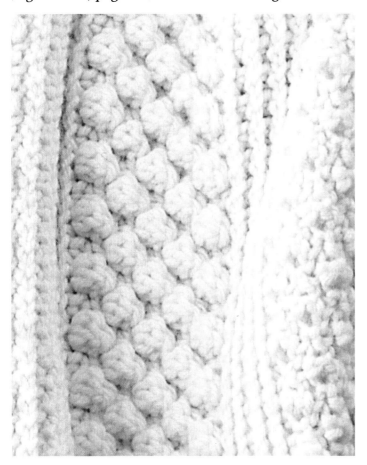

With larger size hook, ch 346.
Row 1 (Right side): Slip st in second ch from hook, (ch 1, skip next ch, slip st in next ch) across: 345 sts.
Note: Loop a short piece of yarn around any stitch to mark last row as **right** side.
Row 2: Ch 1, turn; working in BLO *(Fig. 18, page 140)*, slip st in first slip st, (ch 1, skip next ch, slip st in next slip st) across.
Row 3: Ch 1, turn; working in BLO, sc in first slip st and in next ch, (ch 1, skip next slip st, sc in next ch) across to last slip st, sc in last slip st.
Row 4: Ch 1, turn; working in BLO, slip st in first sc, (ch 1, skip next st, slip st in next ch) across to last 2 sc, ch 1, skip next sc, slip st in last sc.
Rows 5-9: Repeat Rows 3 and 4 twice, then repeat Row 3 once **more**.
Row 10: Ch 1, turn; working in BLO, slip st in first sc, dc in next sc, ★ slip st in next ch, (ch 1, skip next sc, slip st in next ch) twice, dc in next sc; repeat from ★ across to last sc, slip st in last sc: 58 dc.
Row 11: Ch 1, turn; working in FLO, slip st in first slip st, (ch 1, skip next st, slip st in next slip st) across.
Row 12: Ch 1, turn; working in BLO, slip st in first slip st, dc in next ch, slip st in next slip st, ★ (ch 1, skip next ch, slip st in next slip st) twice, dc in next ch, slip st in next slip st; repeat from ★ across.
Rows 13-21: Repeat Rows 11 and 12, 4 times; then repeat Row 11 once **more**.
Rows 22-29: Repeat Rows 2-9.
Row 30: Ch 1, turn; working in BLO, sc in first sc, ch 1, skip next sc, dc in next ch, ch 1, ★ skip next sc, slip st in next ch, ch 1, skip next sc, dc in next ch, ch 1; repeat from ★ across to last 2 sc, skip next sc, sc in last sc: 86 dc.
Row 31: Ch 1, turn; working in FLO, slip st in first sc, (ch 1, skip next st, slip st in next st) across.
Row 32: Ch 1, turn; working in BLO, sc in first slip st, ch 1, skip next ch, slip st in next slip st, ch 1, ★ skip next ch, dc in next slip st, ch 1, skip next ch, slip st in next slip st, ch 1; repeat from ★ across to last 2 sts, skip next ch, sc in last slip st: 85 dc.
Row 33: Ch 1, turn; working in FLO, slip st in first sc, (ch 1, skip next ch, slip st in next st) across.

Row 34: Ch 1, turn; working in BLO, sc in first slip st, ch 1, skip next ch, dc in next slip st, ch 1, ★ skip next ch, slip st in next slip st, ch 1, skip next ch, dc in next slip st, ch 1; repeat from ★ across to last 2 sts, skip next ch, sc in last slip st: 86 dc.

Rows 35-43: Repeat Rows 31-34 twice, then repeat Row 31 once **more**.

Rows 44-51: Repeat Rows 2-9.

Row 52: Ch 1, turn; working in BLO, slip st in first sc, work Cluster in next sc, slip st in next ch, ch 1, ★ skip next sc, slip st in next ch, work Cluster in next sc, slip st in next ch, ch 1; repeat from ★ across to last 2 sc, skip next sc, slip st in last sc: 86 Clusters.

Row 53: Ch 1, turn; working in FLO, slip st in first slip st, (ch 1, skip next st, slip st in next slip st) across.

Row 54: Ch 1, turn; working in BLO, slip st in first slip st, ★ ch 1, skip next ch, slip st in next slip st, work Cluster in next ch, slip st in next slip st; repeat from ★ across.

Row 55: Ch 1, turn; working in FLO, slip st in first slip st, (ch 1, skip next st, slip st in next slip st) across.

Row 56: Ch 1, turn; working in BLO, slip st in first slip st, (work Cluster in next ch, slip st in next slip st, ch 1, skip next ch, slip st in next slip st) across.

Rows 57-61: Repeat Rows 53-56 once, then repeat Row 53 once **more**.

Rows 62-69: Repeat Rows 2-9.

Rows 70-83: Repeat Rows 30-43.

Rows 84-103: Repeat Rows 2-21.

Rows 104-111: Repeat Rows 2-9.

Rows 112-116: Repeat Rows 52-56.

Rows 117-123: Repeat Rows 53-56 once, then repeat Rows 53-55 once **more**.

Rows 124-233: Repeat Rows 2-111.
Finish off.

Change to smaller size hook.

Last Row - First Edging: With **right** side facing and working in **both** loops, join yarn with slip st in first sc; (slip st in next sc, ch 1, skip next ch) across to last 2 sc, slip st in last 2 sc; finish off.

Second Edging: With **right** side facing and working in free loops of beginning ch **(Fig. 19b, page 140)**, join yarn with slip st in first ch; (slip st in next ch, ch 1, skip next ch) across to last 2 chs, slip st in last 2 chs; finish off.

Add fringe **(Figs. 25a & b, page 142)**.

STAINED GLASS BEAUTY

*The rows of colorful clusters in this afghan bring to mind
the beauty of stained glass windows.*

Finished Size: Approximately 49″ x 70″

MATERIALS
    Worsted Weight Yarn, approximately:
        MC - 25 ounces, (710 grams)
        CC - 43 ounces, (1,220 grams) **total**
    Crochet hook size G (4.00 mm) **or** size needed for
      gauge

GAUGE: In pattern, 3 Clusters = 2″

CLUSTER
★ YO, insert hook in stitch indicated, YO and pull up a loop, YO and draw through 2 loops on hook; repeat from ★ 2 times **more**, YO and draw through all 4 loops on hook **(Figs. 9a & b, page 135)**.

With MC, ch 152 **loosely**.

Row 1: Sc in second ch from hook and in each ch across, changing to CC in last sc **(Fig. 21, page 141)**; cut MC: 151 sc.

Row 2: Ch 4 **(counts as first dc plus ch 1)**, turn; ★ skip next sc, work Cluster in next sc, ch 1; repeat from ★ across to last 2 sc, skip next sc, dc in last sc changing to MC; cut CC: 74 Clusters.

Row 3: Ch 1, turn; sc in first dc, work Long sc in skipped sc of last MC row **(Fig. 4, page 133)**, ★ sc in top of next Cluster, work Long sc in skipped sc of last MC row (between Clusters); repeat from ★ across to last dc, sc in last dc changing to CC; cut MC.

Repeat Rows 2 and 3 until afghan measures approximately 70″, ending by working a MC row. Finish off.

WARM AUTUMN WRAP

When the cool days of autumn arrive, you'll be warm and cozy
wrapped in this pretty scalloped afghan.

Finished Size: Approximately 46″ x 60″

MATERIALS

Worsted Weight Yarn, approximately:
MC (Terra Cotta) - 13 ounces,
(370 grams, 855 yards)
Color A (Dark Terra Cotta) - 11½ ounces,
(330 grams, 755 yards)
Color B (Light Terra Cotta) - 9½ ounces,
(270 grams, 625 yards)
Crochet hook, size I (5.50 mm) **or** size needed for
gauge

GAUGE: In pattern, sc, (ch 1, sc) 13 times = 6½″
13 rows = 6″
Gauge Swatch: (6½″ x 6″)
Ch 26 **loosely**.
Work same as Afghan for 13 rows.
Finish off.

PATTERN STITCHES

SHELL
(Tr, ch 1) 4 times in space indicated.
V-ST
(Dc, ch 1, dc) in stitch indicated.

STRIPE SEQUENCE

3 Rows Color A *(Fig. 21, page 141)*, 4 rows MC,
4 rows Color B, 4 rows MC, ★ 4 rows Color A,
4 rows MC, 4 rows Color B, 4 rows MC; repeat
from ★ 6 times **more**, 2 rows Color A.

With Color A, ch 194 **loosely**.
Row 1: Sc in second ch from hook and in next ch,
ch 1, (skip next ch, sc in next ch, ch 1) across to last
3 chs, skip next ch, sc in last 2 chs: 98 sc.
Row 2 (Right side): Ch 1, turn; sc in first sc, ch 1, skip
next sc, sc in next ch-1 sp, ch 1, skip next ch-1 sp, work
Shell in next ch-1 sp, ★ skip next ch-1 sp, (sc in next
ch-1 sp, ch 1) 3 times, skip next ch-1 sp, work Shell in
next ch-1 sp; repeat from ★ across to last 2 ch-1 sps,
skip next ch-1 sp, sc in last ch-1 sp, ch 1, skip next sc,
sc in last sc: 16 Shells.
Note: Loop a short piece of yarn around any stitch to
mark last row as **right** side.
Row 3: Ch 1, turn; sc in first sc, ★ dc in next sc, ch 1,
dc in next tr, ch 1, (work V-St in next tr, ch 1) twice, dc

in next tr, ch 1, dc in next sc, sc in next sc; repeat from
★ across.
Note: Work decrease as follows: YO 3 times, insert
hook in next dc, YO and pull up a loop, (YO and draw
through 2 loops on hook) 3 times, skip next sc,
YO 3 times, insert hook in next dc, YO and pull up a
loop, (YO and draw through 2 loops on hook) 3 times,
YO and draw through all 3 loops on hook.
Row 4: Ch 4, turn; dtr in next dc, tr in next dc, ch 1, dc
in next dc, ch 1, (sc in next dc, ch 1) twice, dc in next dc,
ch 1, tr in next dc, ★ decrease, tr in next dc, ch 1, dc in
next dc, ch 1, (sc in next dc, ch 1) twice, dc in next dc,
ch 1, tr in next dc; repeat from ★ across to last ch-1 sp,
YO 3 times, insert hook in next dc, YO and pull up a
loop, (YO and draw through 2 loops on hook) 3 times,
YO 3 times, insert hook in last sc, YO and pull up a
loop, (YO and draw through 2 loops on hook) 3 times,
YO and draw through all 3 loops on hook.
Row 5: Ch 1, turn; sc in first st and in next tr, (ch 1,
skip next ch-1 sp, sc in next st) 5 times, ★ ch 1, skip
next decrease, sc in next st, (ch 1, skip next ch-1 sp, sc
in next st) 5 times; repeat from ★ across to last st, sc in
last st: 98 sc.
Rows 6-129: Repeat Rows 2-5, 31 times.
Do **not** finish off.

EDGING

Rnd 1: Ch 1, turn; (sc, ch 2, sc) in first sc, (ch 1, sc in
next ch-1 sp) across to last 2 sc, ch 1, skip next sc, (sc,
ch 2, sc) in last sc; working in end of rows, ch 1, skip
first row, [(sc, ch 1, sc) in next row, ch 1, skip next
row, sc in next row, ch 1, skip next row] across; (sc,
ch 2, sc) in free loop of first ch *(Fig. 19b, page 140)*;
ch 1, working over beginning ch, (sc in next ch-sp,
ch 1) across to last ch, (sc, ch 2, sc) in free loop of last
ch; working in end of rows, ch 1, skip first row, [sc in
next row, ch 1, skip next row, (sc, ch 1, sc) in next row,
ch 1, skip next row] across; join with slip st to first sc.
Rnd 2: (Slip st, ch 2, slip st) in first ch-2 sp, ch 1, (slip st
in next ch-1 sp, ch 1) across to next corner ch-2 sp,
(slip st, ch 2, slip st) in corner ch-2 sp, ch 2, (slip st in
next ch-1 sp, ch 2) across to next corner ch-2 sp, (slip st,
ch 2, slip st) in corner ch-2 sp, ch 1, (slip st in next
ch-1 sp, ch 1) across to next corner ch-2 sp, (slip st,
ch 2, slip st) in corner ch-2 sp, ch 2, (slip st in next
ch-2 sp, ch 2) across; join with slip st to first st,
finish off.

FALL SPLENDOR

*Fashioned with diagonal stripes of clusters in deep fall colors, this
rich afghan captures the splendor of the season.*

Finished Size: Approximately 43" x 72"

MATERIALS
Worsted Weight Yarn, approximately:
  MC (Dark Green) - 20 ounces,
    (570 grams, 1,315 yards)
  Color A (Gold) - 17 ounces,
    (480 grams, 1,120 yards)
  Color B (Burgundy) - 17 ounces,
    (480 grams, 1,120 yards)
  Crochet hook, size N (10.00 mm) **or** size needed for
    gauge

GAUGE: In pattern, 15 sts and 9 rows = 5"

PATTERN STITCHES

CLUSTER
Working from **front** to **back** around post of next st
(Fig. 13a, page 137), (YO, insert hook around post of
st and pull up a loop, YO and draw through 2 loops on
hook) 3 times, YO and draw through all 4 loops on
hook.

FRONT POST DC (abbreviated FPdc)
YO, insert hook from **front** to **back** around post of
next st and pull up a loop even with last st made
(Fig. 13c, page 137), (YO and draw through 2 loops on
hook) twice.

BEGINNING DECREASE
YO, insert hook in same st and pull up a loop, YO and
draw through 2 loops on hook, YO, insert hook in next
dc and pull up a loop, YO and draw through 2 loops on
hook, YO and draw through all 3 loops on hook.

END DECREASE
(YO, insert hook in **next** dc and pull up a loop, YO and
draw through 2 loops on hook) 3 times, YO and draw
through all 4 loops on hook.

STRIPE SEQUENCE
5 Rows Color A *(Fig. 21, page 141)*, ★ 4 rows MC, 4 rows
Color B, 4 rows Color A; repeat from ★ 10 times **more**.

Row 1: With Color A ch 4, 5 dc in fourth ch from
hook: 6 sts.
Row 2 (Right side): Ch 3 **(counts as first dc, now and
throughout)**, turn; 2 dc in same st, (skip next dc, work
Cluster, dc in same st) twice, 2 dc in last st: 9 sts.
Row 3: Ch 3, turn; 2 dc in same st, (skip next st, work
FPdc, dc in same st) across to last 2 dc, dc in next dc,

2 dc in last dc: 12 sts.
Row 4: Ch 3, turn; 2 dc in same st, (skip next dc, work
Cluster, dc in same st) across to last dc, 2 dc in last dc:
15 sts.
Rows 5-49: Repeat Rows 3 and 4, 22 times; then repeat
Row 3 once **more**: 150 sts.
Row 50: Ch 3, turn; 2 dc in same st, (skip next dc,
work Cluster, dc in same st) across to last 3 dc, work
end decrease.
Row 51: Ch 2, turn; work beginning decrease, (skip
next st, work FPdc, dc in same st) across to last 2 dc,
dc in next dc, 2 dc in last dc.
Rows 52-89: Repeat Rows 50 and 51, 19 times.
Row 90: Ch 3, turn; (YO, insert hook in **next** st and
pull up a loop, YO and draw through 2 loops on hook)
twice, YO and draw through all 3 loops on hook, (skip
next dc, work Cluster, dc in same st) across to last
3 sts, work end decrease: 147 sts.
Row 91: Ch 2, turn; work beginning decrease, (skip
next st, work FPdc, dc in same st) across to last 3 sts,
work end decrease: 144 dc.
Rows 92-134: Repeat Rows 90 and 91, 21 times; then
repeat Row 90 once **more**: 15 sts.
Row 135: Ch 3, turn; (YO, insert hook in **next** st and
pull up a loop, YO and draw through 2 loops on hook)
3 times, YO and draw through all 4 loops on hook,
(skip next st, work FPdc, dc in same st) across to last
3 sts, work end decrease: 11 sts.
Row 136: Ch 3, turn; (YO, insert hook in **next** st and
pull up a loop, YO and draw through 2 loops on hook)
twice, YO and draw through all 3 loops on hook, (skip
next dc, work Cluster, dc in same st) twice, skip next
st, work end decrease: 7 sts.
Row 137: Ch 3, turn; (YO, insert hook in **next** st and
pull up a loop, YO and draw through 2 loops on hook)
5 times, YO and draw through all 6 loops on hook,
leave last st unworked; finish off.

EDGING

Rnd 1: With **right** side facing, join MC with slip st in
top right corner; sc evenly around, working 3 sc in
each corner; join with slip st to first sc.
Rnds 2-4: Ch 2 **(counts as first hdc)**, turn; hdc in next st
and in each st around, working 3 hdc in each corner st;
join with slip st to first hdc.
Rnd 5: Ch 1, turn; sc in each hdc around, working 3 sc
in each corner hdc; join with slip st to first sc, finish off.

PLAID WINNER

Whether you're planning a trip to the stadium or adding a decorative touch to your home, this blanket offers winning style. The plaid look is achieved by weaving double strands of yarn through the mesh background. Crocheted in varsity colors, this afghan also makes a great gift for a student.

Finished Size: Approximately 46″ x 58″

MATERIALS
Worsted Weight Yarn, approximately:
MC - 25 ounces, (710 grams, 1,680 yards)
CC - 11 ounces, (310 grams, 720 yards)
Crochet hook, size F (3.75 mm) **or** size needed for gauge
Yarn needle

GAUGE: In pattern, 8 ch-1 sps and 8 rows = 4″

Note: Blanket is a dc mesh, with two strands of yarn woven through to form the plaid. The ends are knotted to form the fringe.

STRIPE SEQUENCE
8 Rows MC *(Fig. 21, page 141)*, (4 rows CC, 8 rows MC) 9 times.

BLANKET
With MC, ch 188 **loosely**.
Row 1: Dc in 6th ch from hook, ★ ch 1, skip next ch, dc in next ch; repeat from ★ across: 92 sps.
Row 2: Ch 4 **(counts as first dc plus ch 1, now and throughout)**, turn; ★ dc in next dc, ch 1; repeat from ★ across to last sp, skip next ch, dc in next ch.
Rows 3-116: Repeat Row 2; at end of Row 116 do **not** change colors.
Row 117: With MC, turn; slip st in each dc and in each ch across; finish off.
Weave in all yarn ends.

WEAVING
Each row is woven with two strands of yarn. Cut strands 12″ longer than finished blanket length.
Row 1: Thread yarn needle with 2 strands of MC. Hold blanket horizontally with beginning ch at your right. Leaving a 4″ length of yarn for fringe, insert needle through ch below first ch-1 sp of first row. Working toward last row (left), go down in ch-1 sp of first row and come up in ch-1 sp of next row. Continue weaving up and down in each ch-1 sp across. Run needle through slip st on last row. Pull row of weaving evenly so blanket does not pucker.
Row 2: With MC weave next row in same manner, alternating up and down positions with those of preceding row.
Continue weaving in the following Stripe Sequence:
6 Rows MC, (4 rows CC, 8 rows MC) 7 times.

FRINGE
Working across one end, tie a knot with the first 3 strands (2 strands from the first row and one strand from the second row).
Tie a knot with the next 2 strands (one strand from the second row and one strand from the third row) *(Fig. 26, page 142)*. Continue in this manner until each strand has been used, tying last knot with the last 3 strands.
Lay flat on hard surface and trim ends evenly to 3″ lengths.

AUTUMN LEAVES

Worked holding two strands of yarn together as you go, this warm throw features a scattering of stitches with the look of autumn leaves.

Finished Size: Approximately 48″ x 59″

MATERIALS
Worsted Weight Yarn, approximately:
   MC (Tan) - 32 ounces, (910 grams, 2,020 yards)
   CC (Beige) - 32 ounces, (910 grams, 2,020 yards)
Crochet hook, size K (6.50 mm) **or** size needed for gauge

GAUGE: In pattern, 9 sts and 8 rows = 4″

Note: Entire afghan is worked holding two strands of yarn together.

With MC, ch 108 **loosely**.
Row 1 (Right side): Sc in second ch from hook and in each ch across: 107 sc.
Note: Loop a short piece of yarn around any stitch to mark last row as **right** side.
Row 2: Ch 3 **(counts as first dc, now and throughout)**, turn; dc in next sc and in each st across: 107 dc.
Row 3: Ch 1, turn; sc in same st and in each dc across: 107 sc.
Row 4: Ch 3, turn; dc in next sc and in each sc across; finish off: 107 dc..

Note: Work Leaf as follows: working **below** next dc, insert hook in sc one row **below** and two sts to the **right**, YO and pull up a loop *(Fig. 11a, page 136)*, insert hook in dc two rows **below** and one st to the **right**, YO and pull up a loop, insert hook in sc three rows **below**, YO and pull up a loop, insert hook in dc two rows **below** and one st to the **left**, YO and pull up a loop, insert hook in sc one row **below** and two sts to the **left**, YO and pull up a loop, YO and draw through all 6 loops on hook *(Fig. 11b, page 136)*.
Row 5: With **right** side facing, join CC with slip st in first dc; ch 1, sc in same st and in next 4 dc, work Leaf, skip dc under Leaf, ★ sc in next 7 dc, work Leaf, skip dc under Leaf; repeat from ★ across to last 5 dc, sc in last 5 dc: 13 Leaves.
Row 6: Ch 3, turn; dc in next st and in each st across: 107 dc.
Row 7: Ch 1, turn; sc in same st and in each dc across.
Row 8: Ch 3, turn; dc in next sc and in each sc across; finish off.
Row 9: With **right** side facing, join MC with slip st in first dc; ch 1, sc in same st and in next 8 dc, work Leaf, skip dc under Leaf, ★ sc in next 7 dc, work Leaf, skip dc under Leaf; repeat from ★ across to last 9 dc, sc in last 9 dc: 107 sts.
Repeat Rows 2-9 until Afghan measures approximately 58½″, ending by working Row 5; finish off.

EDGING

With **right** side facing and working in free loops of beginning ch *(Fig. 19b, page 140)*, join CC with slip st in first ch; ch 1, sc in same st and in each ch across; finish off.

EVERGREENS IN AUTUMN

Combining the rich colors of evergreen trees and autumn leaves,
this zig-zag patterned afghan is quick and easy to make.

Finished Size: Approximately 48" x 63"

MATERIALS

Worsted Weight Yarn, approximately:

MC (Green) - 27 ounces, (770 grams, 1,697 yards)

CC (Rust) - 24 ounces, (680 grams, 1,509 yards)

Crochet hook, size N (10.00 mm) **or** size needed for gauge

GAUGE: In pattern, 12 sts and 6 rows = 5"

Note #1: Entire afghan is worked holding two strands of yarn together.

Note #2: When changing colors **(Fig. 21, page 141)**, do **not** cut old color. Carry yarn loosely along edge of work; work over loose strands when working Rnd 1 of Edging.

With CC, ch 108 **loosely**.

Row 1 (Wrong side): Sc in second ch from hook, hdc in next ch, dc in next ch, skip next 3 chs, sc in next ch, ★ [ch 4, sc in second ch from hook, hdc in next ch, dc in next ch **(Point made)**], skip next 3 chs, sc in next ch; repeat from ★ across changing to MC in last sc: 26 Points.

Row 2: Ch 4 **(counts as first tr, now and throughout)**, turn; dc in next dc, hdc in next hdc, sc in next sc, ★ tr in next sc, dc in next dc, hdc in next hdc, sc in next sc; repeat from ★ across: 104 sts.

Row 3: Turn; work Point, sc in next tr, (work Point, sc in next tr) across changing to CC in last sc.

Row 4: Ch 4, turn; dc in next dc, hdc in next hdc, sc in next sc, ★ tr in next sc, dc in next dc, hdc in next hdc, sc in next sc; repeat from ★ across.

Row 5: Turn; work Point, sc in next tr, (work Point, sc in next tr) across changing to MC in last sc.

Row 6: Ch 4, turn; dc in next dc, hdc in next hdc, sc in next sc, ★ tr in next sc, dc in next dc, hdc in next hdc, sc in next sc; repeat from ★ across.

Row 7: Turn; work Point, sc in next tr, (work Point, sc in next tr) across changing to CC in last sc.

Row 8: Ch 4, turn; dc in next dc, hdc in next hdc, sc in next sc, ★ tr in next sc, dc in next dc, hdc in next hdc, sc in next sc; repeat from ★ across.

Rows 9-72: Repeat Rows 5-8, 16 times.

Finish off.

EDGING

Rnd 1: With **right** side facing, join MC with slip st in first tr; ch 1, 3 sc in same st, sc in next st and in each st across to last st, 3 sc in last st; working in end of rows, sc in same row, 3 sc in next row, (sc in next row, 3 sc in next row) across; working in free loops of beginning ch **(Fig. 19b, page 140)**, 3 sc in corner ch (third ch before next sc), sc in next st and in each st across to last st, 3 sc in last st; working in end of rows, sc in same row, 3 sc in next row, (sc in next row, 3 sc in next row) across; join with slip st to first sc: 504 sc.

Rnd 2: Ch 1, do **not** turn; sc in same st, work Point, skip next 3 sc, ★ sc in next sc, work Point, skip next 3 sc; repeat from ★ around; join with slip st to first sc, finish off: 126 Points.

PRETTY PANELS

Pretty openwork panels linked by eye-catching cables characterize this autumn afghan crocheted with brushed acrylic yarn.

Finished Size: Approximately 44″ x 59″

MATERIALS

Worsted Weight Brushed Acrylic Yarn,
approximately:
  30 ounces, (850 grams, 2,315 yards)
Crochet hook, size J (6.00 mm) **or** size needed for gauge

GAUGE: 12 dc and 7 rows = 4″
  In Shell pattern, 12 sts and 8 rows = 4″

Note: Afghan is worked from side to side.

Ch 183 **loosely**.
Row 1: Sc in second ch from hook and in each ch across: 182 sc.
Row 2 (Right side)**:** Turn; slip st **loosely** in Front Loop Only of each sc across *(Fig. 18, page 140)*.
Row 3: Ch 1, turn; working in free loops on previous row *(Fig. 19a, page 140)*, sc in each sc across.
Row 4: Ch 1, turn; sc in first sc, ch 3 **loosely**, skip next 2 sc, sc in next sc *(Fig. 8a, page 135)*, **turn**, sc in each ch just completed *(Fig. 8b, page 135)*, slip st in next sc (sc before ch was begun) *(Fig. 8c, page 135)*, **turn**, working **behind** ch-3, sc in 2 skipped sc *(Fig. 8d, page 135, **first Cable made**)*, ★ ch 3 **loosely**, skip sc where previous ch was attached and next 2 sc, sc in next sc, **turn**, sc in each ch just completed, slip st in next sc (sc before ch was begun), **turn**, working **behind** ch-3, sc in 2 skipped sc **(Cable made)**; repeat from ★ across to last sc, sc in last sc: 60 Cables.
Row 5: Ch 1, turn; sc in first sc, ★ 2 sc in next sc (behind Cable), sc in next sc (behind same Cable), skip sc where ch is attached; repeat from ★ across to last sc, sc in last sc: 182 sc.
Row 6: Turn; slip st **loosely** in Front Loop Only of each sc across.
Row 7: Ch 1, turn; working in free loops on previous row, sc in each sc across.
Row 8: Ch 3 **(counts as first dc, now and throughout)**, turn; dc in next 19 sc, ch 1, skip next 3 sc, (2 dc, ch 1, 2 dc) **(Shell made)** in next sc, ch 1, skip next 3 sc, ★ dc in next 10 sc, ch 1, skip next 3 sc, work Shell in next sc, ch 1, skip next 3 sc; repeat from ★ 8 times **more**, dc in last 2 sc: 10 Shells.

Row 9 AND ALL WRONG SIDE ROWS
through Row 19: Ch 1, turn; sc in first dc, sc in each dc and in each ch-1 sp across: 182 sc.
Row 10: Ch 3, turn; dc in next 16 sc, ch 1, skip next 3 sc, work Shell in next sc, ch 1, skip next 3 sc, ★ dc in next 10 sc, ch 1, skip next 3 sc, work Shell in next sc, ch 1, skip next 3 sc; repeat from ★ 8 times **more**, dc in last 5 sc.
Row 12: Ch 3, turn; dc in next 13 sc, ch 1, skip next 3 sc, work Shell in next sc, ch 1, skip next 3 sc, ★ dc in next 10 sc, ch 1, skip next 3 sc, work Shell in next sc, ch 1, skip next 3 sc; repeat from ★ 8 times **more**, dc in last 8 sc.
Row 14: Ch 3, turn; ★ dc in next 10 sc, ch 1, skip next 3 sc, work Shell in next sc, ch 1, skip next 3 sc; repeat from ★ 9 times **more**, dc in last 11 sc.
Row 16: Ch 3, turn; dc in next 7 sc, ch 1, skip next 3 sc, work Shell in next sc, ch 1, skip next 3 sc, ★ dc in next 10 sc, ch 1, skip next 3 sc, work Shell in next sc, ch 1, skip next 3 sc; repeat from ★ 8 times **more**, dc in last 14 sc.
Row 18: Ch 3, turn; dc in next 4 sc, ch 1, skip next 3 sc, work Shell in next sc, ch 1, skip next 3 sc, ★ dc in next 10 sc, ch 1, skip next 3 sc, work Shell in next sc, ch 1, skip next 3 sc; repeat from ★ 8 times **more**, dc in last 17 sc.
Row 20: Ch 3, turn; dc in next sc, ch 1, skip next 3 sc, work Shell in next sc, ch 1, skip next 3 sc, ★ dc in next 10 sc, ch 1, skip next 3 sc, work Shell in next sc, ch 1, skip next 3 sc; repeat from ★ 8 times **more**, dc in last 20 sc.
Row 21: Ch 1, turn; sc in first dc, sc in each dc and in each ch-1 sp across.
Rows 22-27: Repeat Rows 2-7.
Rows 28 and 29: Repeat Rows 20 and 21.
Rows 30 and 31: Repeat Rows 18 and 19.
Rows 32 and 33: Repeat Rows 16 and 17.
Rows 34 and 35: Repeat Rows 14 and 15.
Rows 36 and 37: Repeat Rows 12 and 13.
Rows 38 and 39: Repeat Rows 10 and 11.
Rows 40 and 41: Repeat Rows 8 and 9.
Rows 42-127: Repeat Rows 2-41 twice, then repeat Rows 2-7 once **more**.

EDGING

Ch 1, turn; sc evenly around, working 3 sc in each corner; join with slip st to first sc, finish off.

RUSTIC RIPPLE

*If you're in the market for an afghan that's quick to make,
look no more! This rustic ripple afghan works up in a jiffy because
you hold two strands of yarn together as you crochet.*

Finished Size: Approximately 48″ x 62″

MATERIALS
  Worsted Weight Yarn, approximately:
    MC (Ecru) - 31 ounces, (880 grams, 1,950 yards)
    Color A (Green) - 12 ounces,
      (340 grams, 755 yards)
    Color B (Rust) - 12 ounces, (340 grams, 755 yards)
  Crochet hook, size P (12.00 mm) **or** size needed for
    gauge

GAUGE: In pattern, 2 repeats = 16″ and 4 rows = 4″
    Gauge Swatch: (16″ x 4″)
    Ch 40 **loosely**.
    Work same as Afghan for 4 rows.
    Finish off.

Note: Entire afghan is worked holding two strands of
yarn together.

With MC, ch 116 **loosely**.
Row 1 (Right side): Dc in fifth ch from hook and in
next 6 chs, (dc, ch 2, dc) in next ch, ★ dc in next 8 chs,
skip next 2 chs, dc in next 8 chs, (dc, ch 2, dc) in next
ch; repeat from ★ across to last 9 chs, dc in next 7 chs,
skip next ch, dc in last ch.

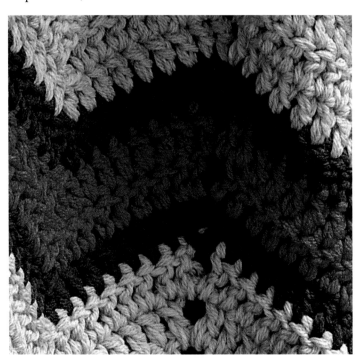

Row 2: Ch 3 **(counts as first dc, now and throughout)**,
turn; skip next dc, dc in next 7 dc, (dc, ch 2, dc) in next
ch-2 sp, ★ dc in next 8 dc, skip next 2 dc, dc in next 8 dc,
(dc, ch 2, dc) in next ch-2 sp; repeat from ★ across to
last 9 sts, dc in next 7 dc, skip next dc, dc in top of
beginning ch: 108 dc.
Rows 3 and 4: Ch 3, turn; skip next dc, dc in next 7 dc,
(dc, ch 2, dc) in next ch-2 sp, ★ dc in next 8 dc, skip next
2 dc, dc in next 8 dc, (dc, ch 2, dc) in next ch-2 sp;
repeat from ★ across to last 9 dc, dc in next 7 dc, skip
next dc, dc in last dc; at end of Row 4 finish off.
Row 5: With **right** side facing, join Color A with slip st
in first dc; ch 3, skip next dc, dc in next 7 dc, (dc, ch 2,
dc) in next ch-2 sp, ★ dc in next 8 dc, skip next 2 dc, dc
in next 8 dc, (dc, ch 2, dc) in next ch-2 sp; repeat from ★
across to last 9 dc, dc in next 7 dc, skip next dc, dc in
last dc; finish off.
Row 6: With **wrong** side facing, join Color B with
slip st in first dc; ch 3, skip next dc, dc in next 7 dc,
(dc, ch 2, dc) in next ch-2 sp, ★ dc in next 8 dc, skip next
2 dc, dc in next 8 dc, (dc, ch 2, dc) in next ch-2 sp;
repeat from ★ across to last 9 dc, dc in next 7 dc, skip
next dc, dc in last dc.
Row 7: Ch 3, turn; skip next dc, dc in next 7 dc, (dc,
ch 2, dc) in next ch-2 sp, ★ dc in next 8 dc, skip next
2 dc, dc in next 8 dc, (dc, ch 2, dc) in next ch-2 sp;
repeat from ★ across to last 9 dc, dc in next 7 dc, skip
next dc, dc in last dc; finish off.
Row 8: With **wrong** side facing, join Color A with
slip st in first dc; ch 3, skip next dc, dc in next 7 dc,
(dc, ch 2, dc) in next ch-2 sp, ★ dc in next 8 dc, skip next
2 dc, dc in next 8 dc, (dc, ch 2, dc) in next ch-2 sp;
repeat from ★ across to last 9 dc, dc in next 7 dc, skip
next dc, dc in last dc; finish off.
Row 9: With **right** side facing, join MC with slip st in
first dc; ch 3, skip next dc, dc in next 7 dc, (dc, ch 2, dc)
in next ch-2 sp, ★ dc in next 8 dc, skip next 2 dc, dc in
next 8 dc, (dc, ch 2, dc) in next ch-2 sp; repeat from ★
across to last 9 dc, dc in next 7 dc, skip next dc, dc in
last dc.
Rows 10-12: Ch 3, turn; skip next dc, dc in next 7 dc,
(dc, ch 2, dc) in next ch-2 sp, ★ dc in next 8 dc, skip next
2 dc, dc in next 8 dc, (dc, ch 2, dc) in next ch-2 sp;
repeat from ★ across to last 9 dc, dc in next 7 dc, skip
next dc, dc in last dc; at end of Row 12 finish off.
Rows 13-60: Repeat Rows 5-12, 6 times.

STITCH SAMPLER

You can use your scrap yarn to make this unique throw,
which features a sampling of delightful stitches.

Finished Size: Approximately 61" x 61"

MATERIALS
Worsted Weight Yarn, approximately:
Color A (Ecru) - 9 ounces, (260 grams, 595 yards)
Color B (Terra Cotta) - 7½ ounces,
(210 grams, 495 yards)
Color C (Teal) - 7 ounces, (200 grams, 460 yards)
Color D (Navy) - 5 ounces, (140 grams, 330 yards)
Color E (Green) - 5 ounces, (140 grams, 330 yards)
Color F (Dark Brown) - 5 ounces,
(140 grams, 330 yards)
Color G (Brown) - 5 ounces,
(140 grams, 330 yards)
Color H (Taupe) - 4½ ounces,
(130 grams, 295 yards)
Color I (Light Terra Cotta) - ½ ounce,
(15 grams, 35 yards)
Crochet hook, size H (5.00 mm) **or** size needed for gauge

GAUGE: Rnds 1-4 = 4"

Rnd 1 (Right side): With Color I, ch 4, 13 dc in fourth ch from hook; join with slip st to top of beginning ch: 14 sts.
Note: Loop a short piece of yarn around any stitch to mark last round as **right** side.
Rnd 2: Ch 1, 2 sc in same st, sc in next dc, (2 sc in next dc, sc in next dc) around; join with slip st to first sc: 21 sc.
Rnd 3: Ch 4, (dc in next sc, ch 1) around; join with slip st to third ch of beginning ch-4, finish off.
Rnd 4: With **right** side facing, join Color A with slip st in same st as joining; ch 1, sc in same st, sc in each ch-1 sp and in each dc around; join with slip st to first sc, finish off: 42 sc.
Rnd 5: With **right** side facing, join Color C with slip st in any sc; ch 3 **(counts as first dc, unless otherwise specified)**, dc in next 2 sc, 2 dc in next sc, (dc in next 4 sc, 2 dc in next sc) twice, ★ dc in next 3 sc, 2 dc in next sc, (dc in next 4 sc, 2 dc in next sc) twice; repeat from ★ around; join with slip st to first dc: 51 dc.
Rnd 6: Ch 1, (sc, ch 2, 2 dc) in same dc, skip next 2 dc, ★ (sc, ch 2, 2 dc) in next dc, skip next 2 dc; repeat from ★ around; join with slip st to first sc: 17 ch-2 sps.
Rnd 7: Slip st in next 2 chs, ch 1, sc in same ch, ch 5, (skip next 3 sts and next ch, sc in next ch, ch 5) around; join with slip st to first sc: 17 loops.
Rnd 8: Ch 1, sc in same sc, 5 sc in first loop, (sc in next sc, 5 sc in next loop) around; join with slip st to first sc: 102 sc.
Rnd 9: Slip st in next 2 sc, ch 1, sc in same sc and in next 2 sc, ch 4, skip next 3 sc, (sc in next 3 sc, ch 4, skip next 3 sc) around; join with slip st to first sc: 17 loops.
Rnd 10: Slip st in next sc, ch 1, sc in same sc, ch 4, sc in next loop, ch 4, (sc in center sc of next 3-sc group, ch 4, sc in next loop, ch 4) around; join with slip st to first sc: 34 loops.
Rnd 11: Slip st in first loop, ch 3, 5 dc in same sp, sc in next loop, (6 dc in next loop, sc in next loop) around; join with slip st to first dc, finish off: 17 6-dc groups.
Rnd 12: With **right** side facing, join Color A with slip st in any sc (between 6-dc groups); ch 3 **(counts as first hdc plus ch 1)**, hdc in same sc, skip next dc, sc in next 4 dc, skip next dc, ★ (hdc, ch 1, hdc) in next sc, skip next dc, sc in next 4 dc, skip next dc; repeat from ★ around; join with slip st to second ch of beginning ch-3: 17 ch-1 sps.
Rnd 13: Ch 1, 2 sc in same st, sc in each ch and in each st around; join with slip st to first sc: 120 sc.
Rnd 14: Ch 3 **(counts as first hdc plus ch 1)**, hdc in same sc, sc in next 29 sc, ★ (hdc, ch 1, hdc) in next sc, sc in next 29 sc; repeat from ★ around; join with slip st to second ch of beginning ch-3: 31 sts **each** side.
Rnd 15: Ch 3, dc in same st, ★ † (dc, ch 2, dc) in next ch-1 sp, dc in next 5 sts, hdc in next 6 sc, sc in next 9 sc, hdc in next 6 sc, dc in next 4 sc †, 2 dc in next hdc; repeat from ★ 2 times **more**, then repeat from † to † once; join with slip st to first dc: 34 sts **each** side.
Rnd 16: Ch 3, dc in next dc, ★ † tr in next dc, (tr, ch 2, tr) in next ch-2 sp, tr in next dc, dc in next 7 sts, hdc in next 4 sts, sc in next 10 sts, hdc in next 4 sts †, dc in next 7 sts; repeat from ★ 2 times **more**, then repeat from † to † once, dc in last 5 sts; join with slip st to first dc: 36 sts **each** side.
Rnd 17: Ch 3, dc in next 2 sts, ★ † tr in next tr, (tr, ch 3, tr) in next ch-2 sp, tr in next tr, dc in next 5 sts, hdc in next 3 sts, sc in next 18 sts, hdc in next 3 sts †, dc in next 5 sts; repeat from ★ 2 times **more**, then repeat from † to † once, dc in last 2 sts; join with slip st to first dc: 38 sts **each** side.
Rnd 18: Ch 2, hdc in next 3 sts, ★ † dc in next tr, (2 dc, ch 3, 2 dc) in next ch-3 sp, dc in next tr, hdc in next

5 sts, sc in next 26 sts †, hdc in next 5 sts; repeat from ★ 2 times **more**, then repeat from † to † once, hdc in last dc; join with slip st to top of beginning ch-2, finish off: 42 sts **each** side.

Rnd 19: With **right** side facing, join Color C with slip st in any corner ch-3 sp; ch 4, hdc in same sp, ★ sc in each st across to next corner ch-3 sp, (hdc, ch 2, hdc) in corner ch-3 sp; repeat from ★ 2 times **more**, sc in each st across; join with slip st to second ch of beginning ch-4: 44 sts **each** side.

Note: Work Cross Stitch as follows: Skip next st, dc in next st, working **around** dc just made, dc in skipped st *(Fig. 10, page 136)*.

Rnd 20: Ch 3, dc in sc to right of beginning ch **(first Cross St made)**, ch 1, (2 dc, ch 2, 2 dc) in first corner ch-2 sp, ★ ch 1, work Cross St, (ch 1, skip next sc, work Cross St) across to next corner ch-2 sp, ch 1, (2 dc, ch 2, 2 dc) in corner ch-2 sp; repeat from ★ 2 times **more**, ch 1, (work Cross St, ch 1, skip next sc) across; join with slip st to first dc: 15 Cross Sts **each** side.

Rnd 21: Ch 1, sc in same dc and in next dc, sc in next ch-1 sp and in next 2 dc, (hdc, ch 3, hdc) in next corner ch-2 sp, ★ sc in each dc and in each ch-1 sp across to next corner ch-2 sp, (hdc, ch 3, hdc) in corner ch-2 sp; repeat from ★ 2 times **more**, sc in each dc and in each ch-1 sp across; join with slip st to first sc, finish off: 52 sts **each** side.

Rnd 22: With **right** side facing, join Color D with slip st in any corner ch-3 sp; ch 5, hdc in same sp, ★ sc in each st across to next corner ch-3 sp, (hdc, ch 3, hdc) in corner ch-3 sp; repeat from ★ 2 times **more**, sc in each st across; join with slip st to second ch of beginning ch-5: 54 sts **each** side.

Rnd 23: Ch 3, dc in sc to right of beginning ch, ch 1, (2 dc, ch 3, 2 dc) in first corner ch-3 sp, ch 1, ★ (skip next st, work Cross St, ch 1) across to next corner ch-3 sp, (2 dc, ch 3, 2 dc) in corner ch-3 sp, ch 1; repeat from ★ 2 times **more**, skip next st, (work Cross St, ch 1, skip next st) across; join with slip st to first dc: 18 Cross Sts **each** side.

Rnd 24: Ch 1, sc in same dc and in next dc, sc in next ch-1 sp and in next 2 dc, (sc, ch 3, sc) in next corner ch-3 sp, ★ sc in each dc and in each ch-1 sp across to next corner ch-3 sp, (sc, ch 3, sc) in corner ch-3 sp; repeat from ★ 2 times **more**, sc in each dc and in each ch-1 sp across; join with slip st to first sc, finish off: 61 sc **each** side.

Rnd 25: With **right** side facing, join Color A with slip st in any corner ch-3 sp; ch 1, (2 sc, ch 3, 2 sc) in same sp, ★ skip next sc, (2 sc in next sc, skip next sc) across to next corner ch-3 sp, (2 sc, ch 3, 2 sc) in corner ch-3 sp; repeat from ★ 2 times **more**, skip next sc, (2 sc in next sc, skip next sc) across; join with slip st to first sc, finish off: 64 sc **each** side.

Rnd 26: With **right** side facing, join Color B with slip st in any corner ch-3 sp; ch 1, (sc, ch 3, sc) in same sp, ★ sc in each sc across to next corner ch-3 sp, (sc, ch 3, sc) in corner ch-3 sp; repeat from ★ 2 times **more**, sc in each sc across; join with slip st to first sc: 66 sc **each** side.

Rnd 27: Slip st in first ch-3 sp, ch 6, dc in same sp, ch 1, skip next sc, (dc, ch 1, dc) in next sc, ★ [skip next 2 sc, (dc, ch 1, dc) in next sc] across to within one sc of next corner ch-3 sp, ch 1, skip next sc, (dc, ch 3, dc) in corner ch-3 sp, ch 1, skip next sc, (dc, ch 1, dc) in next sc; repeat from ★ 2 times **more**, [skip next 2 sc, (dc, ch 1, dc) in next sc] across to last sc, ch 1, skip last sc; join with slip st to third ch of beginning ch-6: 24 ch-1 sps **each** side.

Rnd 28: Ch 3, (dc, ch 3, dc) in first corner ch-3 sp, dc in next dc and in next ch-1 sp, ★ (dc, ch 1, dc) in each ch-1 sp across to within one ch-1 sp of next corner ch-3 sp, dc in next ch-1 sp and in next dc, (dc, ch 3, dc) in corner ch-3 sp, dc in next dc and in next ch-1 sp; repeat from ★ 2 times **more**, (dc, ch 1, dc) in each ch-1 sp across to last ch-1 sp, dc in last ch-1 sp; join with slip st to first dc: 22 ch-1 sps **each** side.

Rnd 29: Ch 1, sc in same st and in next dc, (2 sc, ch 3, 2 sc) in first corner ch-3 sp, ★ sc in each dc and in each ch-1 sp across to next corner ch-3 sp, (2 sc, ch 3, 2 sc) in corner ch-3 sp; repeat from ★ 2 times **more**, sc in each dc and in each ch-1 sp across; join with slip st to first sc, finish off: 76 sc **each** side.

Rnd 30: With **right** side facing, join Color A with slip st in any corner ch-3 sp; ch 1, (sc, ch 3, sc) in same sp, ★ sc in each sc across to next corner ch-3 sp, (sc, ch 3, sc) in corner ch-3 sp; repeat from ★ 2 times **more**, sc in each sc across; join with slip st to first sc: 78 sc **each** side.

Note: Work Shell as follows: (2 Dc, ch 1, 2 dc) in stitch or space indicated.

Rnd 31: Ch 1, sc in same st, work Shell in first corner ch-3 sp, sc in next sc, skip next 2 sc, work Shell in next sc, ★ (skip next 2 sc, sc in next sc, skip next 2 sc, work Shell in next sc) across to within 2 sc of next corner ch-3 sp, skip next sc, sc in next sc, work Shell in corner ch-3 sp, sc in next sc, skip next 2 sc, work Shell in next sc; repeat from ★ 2 times **more**, (skip next 2 sc, sc in next sc, skip next 2 sc, work Shell in next sc) across to last sc, skip last sc; join with slip st to first sc: 56 Shells.

Rnd 32: Ch 5, (hdc, ch 2, hdc) in next Shell (ch-1 sp), ch 2, ★ dc in next sc (between Shells), ch 2, (hdc in next Shell, ch 2, dc in next sc, ch 2) across to next corner Shell, (hdc, ch 2, hdc) in corner Shell, ch 2; repeat from ★ 2 times **more**, (dc in next sc, ch 2, hdc in next Shell, ch 2) across; join with slip st to third ch of beginning ch-5: 28 ch-2 sps **each** side.

Rnd 33: Ch 1, sc in same st, 2 sc in first ch-2 sp, sc in next hdc, (sc, ch 2, sc) in next corner ch-2 sp, ★ sc in next hdc, (2 sc in next ch-2 sp, sc in next st) across to next corner ch-2 sp, (sc, ch 2, sc) in corner ch-2 sp; repeat from ★ 2 times **more**, (sc in next st, 2 sc in next ch-2 sp) across; join with slip st to first sc, finish off: 87 sc **each** side.

Rnd 34: With **right** side facing, join Color D with slip st in any corner ch-2 sp; ch 1, (sc, ch 2, sc) in same sp, ★ sc in each sc across to next corner ch-2 sp, (sc, ch 2, sc) in corner sp; repeat from ★ 2 times **more**, sc in each sc across; join with slip st to first sc, finish off: 89 sc **each** side.

Rnd 35: With **right** side facing, join Color E with slip st in any corner ch-2 sp; ch 1, (sc, ch 2, sc) in same sp, ch 1, ★ skip next sc, (sc in next sc, ch 1, skip next sc) across to next corner ch-2 sp, (sc, ch 2, sc) in corner ch-2 sp, ch 1; repeat from ★ 2 times **more**, skip next sc, (sc in next sc, ch 1, skip next sc) across; join with slip st to first sc: 45 ch-1 sps **each** side.

Rnds 36 and 37: Slip st in first ch-2 sp, ch 1, (sc, ch 2, sc) in same sp, ch 1, ★ (sc in next ch-1 sp, ch 1) across to next corner ch-2 sp, (sc, ch 2, sc) in corner ch-2 sp, ch 1; repeat from ★ 2 times **more**, (sc in next ch-1 sp, ch 1) across; join with slip st to first sc, at end of Row 37 finish off: 47 ch-1 sps **each** side.

Rnd 38: With **right** side facing, join Color H with slip st in any corner ch-2 sp; ch 1, (sc, ch 2, sc) in same sp, ★ sc in each sc and in each ch-1 sp across to next corner ch-2 sp, (sc, ch 2, sc) in corner ch-2 sp; repeat from ★ 2 times **more**, sc in each sc and in each ch-1 sp across; drop yarn, pick up Color C and join with slip st to first sc, do **not** finish off: 97 sc **each** side.

Note: Work Bobble as follows: ★ YO, insert hook in sc indicated, YO and pull up a loop, YO and draw through 2 loops on hook; repeat from ★ 4 times **more**, YO and draw through all 6 loops on hook. Push Bobble to **right** side of work.

Rnd 39: With Color C, ch 1, sc in same st, (sc, ch 2, sc) in first corner ch-2 sp, sc in next 3 sc, work Bobble in next sc, ★ (sc in next 4 sc, work Bobble in next sc) across to within 3 sc of next corner ch-2 sp, sc in next 3 sc, (sc, ch 2, sc) in next corner ch-2 sp, sc in next 3 sc, work Bobble in next sc; repeat from ★ 2 times **more**, (sc in next 4 sc, work Bobble in next sc) across to last 2 sc, sc in last 2 sc; cut Color C, pick up Color H and join with slip st to first sc: 19 Bobbles **each** side.

Rnd 40: With Color H, ch 1, sc in same sc and in next sc, (sc, ch 2, sc) in first corner ch-2 sp, ★ sc in each st across to next corner ch-2 sp, (sc, ch 2, sc) in corner ch-2 sp; repeat from ★ 2 times **more**, sc in each st across; join with slip st to first sc, finish off: 101 sc **each** side.

Rnd 41: With **right** side facing, join Color B with slip st in any corner ch-2 sp; ch 1, (sc, ch 2, sc) in same sp, ★ sc in each sc across to next corner ch-2 sp, (sc, ch 2, sc) in corner ch-2 sp; repeat from ★ 2 times **more**, sc in each sc across; join with slip st to first sc: 103 sc **each** side.

Note: Work Large Shell as follows: (3 Dc, ch 2, 3 dc) in sc indicated.

Rnd 42: Slip st in first ch-2 sp, ch 6, dc in same sp, skip next 3 sc, work Large Shell in next sc, ★ (skip next 2 sc, sc in next sc, skip next 2 sc, work Large Shell in next sc) across to within 3 sc of next corner ch-2 sp, skip next 3 sc, (dc, ch 3, dc) in corner ch-2 sp, skip next 3 sc, work Large Shell in next sc; repeat from ★ 2 times **more**, (skip next 2 sc, sc in next sc, skip next 2 sc, work Large Shell in next sc) across to last 3 sc, skip last 3 sc; join with slip st to third ch of beginning ch-6: 17 Large Shells **each** side.

Rnd 43: Ch 4, dc in same st, ch 1, (dc, ch 2, dc) in next corner ch-3 sp, ch 1, (dc, ch 1, dc) in next dc, ch 1, sc in next Large Shell (ch-2 sp), ch 1, ★ [(dc, ch 1, dc) in next sc (between Large Shells), ch 1, sc in next Large Shell, ch 1] across to within 4 dc of next corner ch-3 sp, skip next 3 dc, (dc, ch 1, dc) in next dc, ch 1, (dc, ch 2, dc) in next corner ch-3 sp, ch 1, (dc, ch 1, dc) in next dc, ch 1, sc in next Large Shell, ch 1; repeat from ★ 2 times **more**, [(dc, ch 1, dc) in next sc, ch 1, sc in next Large Shell, ch 1] across; join with slip st to third ch of beginning ch-4: 54 ch-1 sps **each** side.

Rnd 44: Ch 1, sc in same st, (sc in next ch-1 sp, sc in next dc) twice, (sc, ch 2, sc) in next corner ch-2 sp, ★ sc in each st and in each ch-1 sp across to next corner ch-2 sp, (sc, ch 2, sc) in corner ch-2 sp; repeat from ★ 2 times **more**, sc in each st and in each ch-1 sp across; join with slip st to first sc, finish off: 111 sc **each** side.

Rnd 45: With **right** side facing, join Color F with slip st in any corner ch-2 sp; ch 1, (sc, ch 2, sc) in same sp, 2 sc in next sc, ★ (skip next sc, 2 sc in next sc) across to next corner ch-2 sp, (sc, ch 2, sc) in corner ch-2 sp, 2 sc in next sc; repeat from ★ 2 times **more**, (skip next sc, 2 sc in next sc) across; join with slip st to first sc: 114 sc **each** side.

Rnd 46: Ch 3, (dc, ch 3, dc) in next corner ch-2 sp, dc in next 2 sc, ★ (ch 2, skip next 2 sc, dc in next 2 sc) across to next corner ch-2 sp, (dc, ch 3, dc) in corner ch-2 sp, dc in next 2 dc; repeat from ★ 2 times **more**, ch 2, (skip next 2 sc, dc in next 2 sc, ch 2) across to last 3 sc, skip next 2 sc, dc in last sc; join with slip st to first dc: 60 dc **each** side.

Rnd 47: Ch 1, sc in same st and in next dc, (sc, ch 3, sc) in first corner ch-3 sp, sc in next 3 dc, ★ (2 sc in next ch-2 sp, sc in next 2 dc) across to within one dc of next corner ch-3 sp, sc in next dc, (sc, ch 3, sc) in corner ch-3 sp, sc in next 3 dc; repeat from ★ 2 times **more**, 2 sc in next ch-2 sp, (sc in next 2 dc, 2 sc in next ch-2 sp) across to last dc, sc in last dc; join with slip st to first sc, finish off: 118 sc **each** side.

Rnd 48: With **right** side facing, join Color E with slip st in any corner ch-3 sp; ch 1, (sc, ch 2, sc) in same sp, ★ sc in each sc across to next corner ch-3 sp, (sc, ch 2, sc) in corner ch-3 sp; repeat from ★ 2 times **more**, sc in each sc across; join with slip st to first sc: 120 sc **each** side.

Rnd 49: Ch 1, sc in same st, (hdc, ch 3, hdc) in first

corner ch-2 sp, ★ skip next sc, sc in next sc, (ch 3, skip next sc, sc in next sc) across to next corner ch-2 sp, (hdc, ch 3, hdc) in corner ch-2 sp; repeat from ★ 2 times **more**, skip next sc, (sc in next sc, ch 3, skip next sc) across; join with slip st to first sc: 240 ch-3 sps.

Rnd 50: Slip st in next hdc and in first corner ch-3 sp, ch 1, (sc, ch 3, sc) in same sp, ch 3, ★ (sc in next ch-3 sp, ch 3) across to next corner ch-3 sp, (sc, ch 3, sc) in corner ch-3 sp, ch 3; repeat from ★ 2 times **more**, (sc in next ch-3 sp, ch 3) across; join with slip st to first sc: 244 ch-3 sps.

Rnd 51: Ch 1, sc in same st, (2 sc, ch 2, 2 sc) in first corner ch-3 sp, sc in next sc, ★ 2 sc in each ch-3 sp across to within one sc of next corner ch-3 sp, sc in next sc, (2 sc, ch 2, 2 sc) in next corner ch-3 sp, sc in next sc; repeat from ★ 2 times **more**, 2 sc in each ch-3 sp across; join with slip st to first sc, finish off: 126 sc **each** side.

Rnd 52: With **right** side facing, join Color G with slip st in any corner ch-2 sp; ch 1, (sc, ch 2, sc) in same sp, ★ sc in each sc across to next corner ch-2 sp, (sc, ch 2, sc) in corner ch-2 sp; repeat from ★ 2 times **more**, sc in each sc across; join with slip st to first sc, finish off: 128 sc **each** side.

Note: Work Cluster over next 3 sc as follows: ★ YO, insert hook in **next** sc, YO and pull up a loop, YO and draw through 2 loops on hook; repeat from ★ 2 times **more**, YO and draw through all 4 loops on hook.

Rnd 53: With **right** side facing, join Color H with slip st in any corner ch-2 sp; ch 6, dc in same sp, ch 3, ★ (skip next sc, work Cluster, ch 3) across to next corner ch-2 sp, (dc, ch 3, dc) in corner ch-2 sp, ch 3; repeat from ★ 2 times **more**, (skip next sc, work Cluster, ch 3) across; join with slip st to third ch of beginning ch-6, finish off: 32 Clusters **each** side.

Rnd 54: With **right** side facing, join Color G with slip st in any corner ch-3 sp; ch 1, (sc, ch 2, sc) in same sp, sc in next dc, ★ (3 sc in next ch-3 sp, sc in next st) across to next corner ch-3 sp, (sc, ch 2, sc) in corner ch-3 sp, sc in next dc; repeat from ★ 2 times **more**, (3 sc in next ch-3 sp, sc in next st) across; join with slip st to first sc, finish off: 135 sc **each** side.

Rnd 55: With **right** side facing, join Color A with slip st in any corner ch-2 sp; ch 6, dc in same sp, ★ dc in each sc across to next corner ch-2 sp, (dc, ch 3, dc) in corner ch-2 sp; repeat from ★ 2 times **more**, dc in each sc across; join with slip st to third ch of beginning ch-6, finish off: 137 sts **each** side.

Rnd 56: With **right** side facing, join Color D with slip st in any corner ch-3 sp; ch 1, (sc, ch 2, sc) in same sp, (sc, dc) in next dc, ★ [skip next dc, (sc, dc) in next dc] across to next corner ch-3 sp, (sc, ch 2, sc) in corner ch-3 sp, (sc, dc) in next dc; repeat from ★ 2 times **more**, [skip next dc, (sc, dc) in next dc] across; join with slip st to first sc: 140 sts **each** side.

Rnd 57: Ch 3, sc in same st, (dc, ch 3, dc) in first corner ch-2 sp, (dc, sc) in next sc, ★ (dc in next sc, sc in next dc) across to within one sc of next corner ch-2 sp, (dc, sc) in next sc, (dc, ch 3, dc) in corner ch-2 sp, (dc, sc) in next sc; repeat from ★ 2 times **more**, (dc in next sc, sc in next dc) across; join with slip st to first dc: 144 sts **each** side.

Rnd 58: Ch 1, sc in same st, dc in next 2 sts, (dc, ch 3, dc) in next corner ch-3 sp, dc in next dc, ★ (sc in next dc, dc in next sc) across to within one dc of next corner ch-3 sp, dc in next dc, (dc, ch 3, dc) in corner ch-3 sp, dc in next dc; repeat from ★ 2 times **more**, (sc in next dc, dc in next sc) across; join with slip st to first sc, finish off: 146 sts **each** side.

Rnd 59: With **right** side facing, join Color C with slip st in any corner ch-3 sp; ch 1, (sc, ch 2, sc) in same sp, ★ sc in each st across to next corner ch-3 sp, (sc, ch 2, sc) in corner ch-3 sp; repeat from ★ 2 times **more**, sc in each st across; join with slip st to first sc: 148 sc **each** side.

Note: Work V-St as follows: (Dc, ch 2, dc) in stitch indicated.

Rnd 60: Slip st in first ch-2 sp, ch 7, dc in same sp, skip next 2 sc, work V-St in next sc, ★ (skip next 3 sc, work V-St in next sc) across to within one sc of next corner ch-2 sp, skip next sc, (dc, ch 4, dc) in corner ch-2 sp, skip next 2 sc, work V-St in next sc; repeat from ★ 2 times **more**, (skip next 3 sc, work V-St in next sc) across to last sc, skip last sc; join with slip st to third ch of beginning ch-7: 37 V-Sts **each** side.

Rnd 61: Ch 1, sc in same st, (sc, ch 2, sc) in first corner ch-4 sp, ★ sc in next 2 dc, (2 sc in next ch-2 sp, sc in next 2 dc) across to next corner ch-4 sp, (sc, ch 2, sc) in corner ch-4 sp; repeat from ★ 2 times **more**, (sc in next 2 dc, 2 sc in next ch-2 sp) across to last dc, sc in last dc; join with slip st to first sc, finish off: 152 sc **each** side.

Rnd 62: With **right** side facing, join Color H with slip st in any corner ch-2 sp; ch 6, dc in same sp, ★ dc in each sc across to next corner ch-2 sp, (dc, ch 3, dc) in corner ch-2 sp; repeat from ★ 2 times **more**, dc in each sc across; join with slip st to third ch of beginning ch-6, finish off: 154 sts **each** side.

Note: Work Puff St as follows: (YO, insert hook in dc indicated, YO and pull up a loop even with hook) 3 times, YO and draw through all 7 loops on hook.

Rnd 63: With **right** side facing, join Color G with slip st in first corner ch-3 sp; ch 5, (dc, ch 3, work V-St) in same sp, skip next 2 dc, work Puff St in next dc, ch 1, ★ (skip next 2 dc, work V-St in next dc, skip next 2 dc, work Puff St in next dc, ch 1) across to within one dc of next corner ch-3 sp, skip next dc, work (V-St, ch 3, V-St) in corner ch-3 sp, skip next 2 dc, work Puff St in next dc, ch 1; repeat from ★ 2 times **more**, (skip next 2 dc, work V-St in next dc, skip next 2 dc, work Puff St in next dc, ch 1) across to last st, skip last st; join with slip st to third ch of beginning ch-5: 26 Puff Sts **each** side.

Rnd 64: Ch 1, sc in same st, ★ † sc in next ch-2 sp and in next dc, (sc, ch 2, sc) in first corner ch-3 sp, sc in next dc and in next ch-2 sp †, sc in next 4 sts, (2 sc in next ch-2 sp, sc in next 4 sts) across to within one ch-2 sp of next corner ch-3 sp; repeat from ★ 2 times **more**, then repeat from † to † once, (sc in next 4 sts, 2 sc in next ch-2 sp) across to last 3 sts, sc in last 3 sts; join with slip st to first sc, finish off: 160 sc **each** side.

Rnd 65: With **right** side facing, join Color H with slip st in any corner ch-2 sp; ch 1, (sc, ch 2, sc) in same sp, ch 1, ★ (skip next sc, sc in next sc, ch 1) across to next corner ch-2 sp, (sc, ch 2, sc) in corner ch-2 sp, ch 1; repeat from ★ 2 times **more**, (skip next sc, sc in next sc, ch 1) across; join with slip st to first sc, finish off: 81 ch-1 sps **each** side.

Rnd 66: With **right** side facing, join Color G with slip st in any corner ch-2 sp; ch 1, (sc, ch 2, sc) in same sp, ★ 2 sc in each ch-1 sp across to within one sc of next corner ch-2 sp, sc in next sc, (sc, ch 2, sc) in corner ch-2 sp; repeat from ★ 2 times **more**, 2 sc in each ch-1 sp across to last sc, sc in last sc; join with slip st to first sc, finish off: 165 sc **each** side.

Rnd 67: With **right** side facing, join Color B with slip st in any corner ch-2 sp; ch 1, (sc, ch 2, sc) in same sp, sc in next 2 sc, work Bobble in next sc, ★ (sc in next 4 sc, work Bobble in next sc) across to within 2 sc of next corner ch-2 sp, sc in next 2 sc, (sc, ch 2, sc) in corner ch-2 sp, sc in next 2 sc, work Bobble in next sc; repeat from ★ 2 times **more**, (sc in next 4 sc, work Bobble in next sc) across to last 2 sc, sc in last 2 sc; join with slip st to first sc, finish off: 33 Bobbles **each** side.

Rnd 68: With **right** side facing, join Color G with slip st in any corner ch-2 sp; ch 1, (sc, ch 2, sc) in same sp, ★ sc in each st across to next corner ch-2 sp, (sc, ch 2, sc) in corner ch-2 sp; repeat from ★ 2 times **more**, sc in each st across; join with slip st to first sc: 169 sc **each** side.

Rnd 69: Slip st in first ch-2 sp, ch 1, (sc, ch 2, sc) in same sp, ch 1, skip next sc, ★ (sc in next sc, ch 1, skip next sc) across to next corner ch-2 sp, (sc, ch 2, sc) in corner ch-2 sp, ch 1, skip next sc; repeat from ★ 2 times **more**, (sc in next sc, ch 1, skip next sc) across; join with slip st to first sc, finish off: 85 ch-1 sps **each** side.

Rnd 70: With **right** side facing, join Color A with slip st in any corner ch-2 sp; ch 1, (sc, ch 2, sc) in same sp, ★ sc in each sc and in each ch-1 sp across to next corner ch-2 sp, (sc, ch 2, sc) in corner ch-2 sp; repeat from ★ 2 times **more**, sc in each sc and in each ch-1 sp across; join with slip st to first sc: 173 sc **each** side.

Rnd 71: Ch 3, dc in sc to right of beginning ch, (dc, ch 3, dc) in first corner ch-2 sp, ★ work Cross St, (ch 1, skip next sc, work Cross St) across to next corner ch-2 sp, (dc, ch 3, dc) in corner ch-2 sp; repeat from ★ 2 times **more**, (work Cross St, ch 1, skip next sc) across; join with slip st to first dc:

58 Cross Sts **each** side.

Rnd 72: Ch 1, sc in same st and in next 2 dc, (sc, ch 3, sc) in first corner ch-3 sp, ★ sc in each dc and in each ch-1 sp across to next corner ch-3 sp, (sc, ch 3, sc) in corner ch-3 sp; repeat from ★ 2 times **more**, sc in each dc and in each ch-1 sp across; drop yarn, pick up Color C and join with slip st to first sc, do **not** finish off: 177 sc **each** side.

Rnd 73: With Color C, ch 1, sc in same st, ch 1, skip next sc, sc in next sc, ch 1, skip next sc, (sc, ch 3, sc) in first corner ch-3 sp, ch 1, ★ skip next sc, (sc in next sc, ch 1, skip next sc) across to next corner ch-3 sp, (sc, ch 3, sc) in corner ch-3 sp, ch 1; repeat from ★ 2 times **more**, skip next sc, (sc in next sc, ch 1, skip next sc) across; cut Color C, pick up Color A and join with slip st to first sc: 89 ch-1 sps **each** side.

Rnd 74: With Color A, slip st in first ch-1 sp, ch 1, sc in same sp, ch 1, sc in next ch-1 sp, ch 1, (sc, ch 3, sc) in first corner ch-3 sp, ch 1, ★ (sc in next ch-1 sp, ch 1) across to next corner ch-3 sp, (sc, ch 3, sc) in corner ch-3 sp, ch 1; repeat from ★ 2 times **more**, (sc in next ch-1 sp, ch 1) across; join with slip st to first sc, finish off: 90 ch-1 sps **each** side.

Rnd 75: With **right** side facing, join Color F with slip st in any corner ch-3 sp; ch 1, (sc, ch 2, sc) in same sp, ★ sc in each sc and in each ch-1 sp across to next corner ch-3 sp, (sc, ch 2, sc) in corner ch-3 sp; repeat from ★ 2 times **more**, sc in each sc and in each ch-1 sp across; join with slip st to first sc: 183 sc **each** side.

Rnd 76: Slip st in first ch-2 sp, ch 7, dc in same sp, ch 1, skip next sc, ★ (dc in next sc, ch 1, skip next sc) across to next corner ch-2 sp, (dc, ch 4, dc) in corner ch-2 sp, ch 1, skip next sc; repeat from ★ 2 times **more**, (dc in next sc, ch 1, skip next sc) across; join with slip st to third ch of beginning ch-7: 92 ch-1 sps **each** side.

Rnd 77: Ch 1, sc in same st, (sc, ch 3, sc) in first corner ch-4 sp, ★ sc in each dc and in each ch-1 sp across to next corner ch-4 sp, (sc, ch 3, sc) in corner ch-4 sp; repeat from ★ 2 times **more**, sc in each dc and in each ch-1 sp across; join with slip st to first sc, finish off: 187 sc **each** side.

Rnd 78: With **right** side facing, join Color H with slip st in any corner ch-3 sp; ch 1, (sc, ch 2, sc) in same sp, 2 sc in next sc, ★ (skip next sc, 2 sc in next sc) across to next corner ch-3 sp, (sc, ch 2, sc) in corner ch-3 sp, 2 sc in next sc; repeat from ★ 2 times **more**, (skip next sc, 2 sc in next sc) across; join with slip st to first sc, finish off: 190 sc **each** side.

Rnd 79: With **right** side facing, join Color B with slip st in any corner ch-2 sp; ch 1, (sc, ch 2, sc) in same sp, ★ sc in each sc across to next corner ch-2 sp, (sc, ch 2, sc) in corner ch-2 sp; repeat from ★ 2 times **more**, sc in each sc across; join with slip st to first sc, finish off: 192 sc **each** side.

Rnd 80: With **right** side facing, join Color D with slip st in any corner ch-2 sp; ch 1, (sc, ch 2, sc) in same sp, ★ (ch 1, skip next sc, sc in next sc) across to next corner ch-2 sp, ch 1, (sc, ch 2, sc) in corner ch-2 sp; repeat from ★ 2 times more, (ch 1, skip next sc, sc in next sc) across, ch 1; join with slip st to first sc, finish off: 97 ch-1 sps **each** side.

Rnd 81: With **right** side facing, join Color B with slip st in any corner ch-2 sp; ch 1, (sc, ch 2, sc) in same sp and in each sp around; join with slip st to first sc, finish off: 196 sc **each** side.

AUTUMN SPICE

The warm, subtle hues in this masculine throw are spiced with variegated yarn in shades of cinnamon.

Finished Size: Approximately 49″ x 65″

MATERIALS
Worsted Weight Yarn, approximately:
MC (Grey) - 21 ounces, (600 grams, 1,410 yards)
Color A (Tan) - 17 ounces,
(480 grams, 1,145 yards)
Color B (Variegated) - 16 ounces,
(450 grams, 1,070 yards)
Crochet hook, size K (6.50 mm) **or** size needed for gauge

GAUGE: In pattern, 11 sts = 3¾″
8 rows = 4″
Gauge Swatch: (3¾″ x 4″)
Ch 13 **loosely**.
Work same as Afghan for 8 rows.
Finish off.

STRIPE SEQUENCE
3 Rows MC *(Fig. 21, page 141)*, ★ 4 rows Color A, 4 rows Color B, 4 rows Color A, 4 rows MC, 4 rows Color B, 4 rows MC; repeat from ★ once **more**, 4 rows Color B, 4 rows MC, 4 rows Color A, 4 rows Color B, 4 rows Color A, 4 rows MC, 4 rows Color B, 4 rows MC, 4 rows Color A, 4 rows Color B, 4 rows Color A, 3 rows MC.

Note: Afghan is worked from side to side.

With MC, ch 190 **loosely**.
Row 1: Dc in fourth ch from hook and in each ch across: 188 sts.
Rows 2 and 3: Ch 3 **(counts as first dc, now and throughout)**, turn; dc in next dc and in each dc across.
Note: Work Front Post treble crochet *(abbreviated FPtr)* as follows: YO twice, insert hook from **front** to **back** around post of dc **below** next dc *(Fig. 13d, page 138)*, YO and pull up a loop, (YO and draw through 2 loops on hook) 3 times.
Row 4 (Right side): Ch 1, turn; sc in first 2 dc, (work FPtr, sc in next 2 dc) across: 62 FPtr.
Rows 5-7: Ch 3, turn; dc in next st and in each st across.
Rows 8-98: Repeat Rows 4-7, 22 times; then repeat Rows 4-6 once **more**.
Do **not** finish off.

EDGING
FIRST END
Ch 3, do **not** turn; working in end of rows, dc evenly across; finish off.

SECOND END
With **right** side facing, join MC with slip st in first ch of beginning ch *(Fig. 19b, page 140)*; ch 3, working in end of rows, dc evenly across; finish off.

Add fringe *(Figs. 25a & b, page 142)*.

WINTER

During the winter months, blankets of freshly fallen snow draw many of us outdoors to ski the slopes or just to enjoy the exhilarating air. Others see the frosty weather as a wonderful time to linger indoors, chatting with friends and family by the fireside. The toasty wraps in this section will help keep your conversations cozy, and they're ideal for taking along on your outdoor excursions, too. And don't forget, all of them make perfect Christmas gifts!

A DASH OF RED

There's nothing like a dash of red to brighten the grey days of winter! Crocheted with bulky weight yarn, this sporty afghan is perfect for keeping you warm during your cold-weather outings.

Finished Size: Approximately 49" x 69"

MATERIALS

Bulky Weight Yarn, approximately:
MC (Dark Grey) - 30 ounces,
(850 grams, 1,200 yards)
Color A (Red) - 18 ounces, (510 grams, 720 yards)
Color B (Ecru) - 13 ounces, (370 grams, 520 yards)
Color C (Light Grey) - 12 ounces,
(340 grams, 480 yards)
Crochet hook, size H (5.00 mm) **or** size needed for gauge

GAUGE: 19 dc and 11 rows = 6½"

Note: Afghan is worked from side to side.

With MC, ch 199 **loosely**.
Row 1 (Right side): Dc in fourth ch from hook and in each ch across: 197 sts.
Note: Loop a short piece of yarn around any stitch to mark last row as **right** side.
Rows 2-4: Ch 3 **(counts as first dc, now and throughout)**, turn; dc in next dc and in each st across.
Row 5: Ch 3, turn; dc in next dc and in each dc across changing to Color A in last dc *(Fig. 21, page 141)*; cut MC.
Rows 6-10: Ch 3, turn; dc in next dc and in each dc across changing to Color B in last dc of Row 10; cut Color A.
Note: Do **not** cut yarn unless specified. Carry yarn not being used on **wrong** side, holding it with normal tension.
Row 11: Ch 3, turn; dc in next dc, with MC dc in next dc, ★ with Color B dc in next 3 dc, with MC dc in next dc; repeat from ★ across to last 2 dc, with Color B dc in last 2 dc.
Row 12: Ch 3, turn; ★ with MC dc in next 3 dc, with Color B dc in next dc; repeat from ★ across changing to MC in last dc; cut Color B.
Row 13: Ch 3, turn; dc in next dc, with Color A dc in next dc, ★ with MC dc in next 3 dc, with Color A dc in next dc; repeat from ★ across to last 2 dc, with MC dc in last 2 dc.

Row 14: Ch 3, turn; ★ with Color A dc in next 3 dc, with MC dc in next dc; repeat from ★ across changing to Color C in last dc; cut MC and Color A.
Rows 15-17: Ch 3, turn; dc in next dc and in each dc across changing to MC in last dc of Row 17; cut Color C.
Row 18: Ch 3, turn; ★ with Color A dc in next 3 dc, with MC dc in next dc; repeat from ★ across.
Row 19: Ch 3, turn; dc in next dc, with Color A dc in next dc, ★ with MC dc in next 3 dc, with Color A dc in next dc; repeat from ★ across to last 2 dc, with MC dc in last 2 dc changing to Color B in last dc; cut Color A.
Row 20: Ch 3, turn; ★ with MC dc in next 3 dc, with Color B dc in next dc; repeat from ★ across.
Row 21: Ch 3, turn; dc in next dc, with MC dc in next dc, ★ with Color B dc in next 3 dc, with MC dc in next dc; repeat from ★ across to last 2 dc, with Color B dc in last 2 dc; cut MC.
Row 22: Ch 3, turn; dc in next dc and in each dc across.
Rows 23-68: Repeat Rows 11-22, 3 times; then repeat Rows 11-20 once **more**.
Row 69: Ch 3, turn; dc in next dc, with MC dc in next dc, ★ with Color B dc in next 3 dc, with MC dc in next dc; repeat from ★ across to last 2 dc, with Color B dc in last 2 dc changing to Color A in last dc; cut MC and Color B.
Rows 70-74: Ch 3, turn; dc in next dc and in each dc across changing to MC in last dc of Row 74; cut Color A.
Rows 75-79: Ch 3, turn; dc in next dc and in each dc across; do **not** finish off.

EDGING

Ch 2, working in end of rows, hdc in first row, 2 hdc in next row and in each row across; working in free loops of beginning ch *(Fig. 19b, page 140)*, dc in first ch and in each ch across; working in end of rows, 2 hdc in first row and in each row across; working across Row 79, dc in first dc and in each dc across; join with slip st to top of beginning ch-2, finish off.

Add fringe *(Figs. 25a & b, page 142)*.

ENGLISH GARDEN

*Abloom with color, this mile-a-minute afghan brings the charm
of an English rose garden to cold winter days.*

Finished Size: Approximately 53″ x 72″

MATERIALS
   Worsted Weight Yarn, approximately:
      Color A (Light Rose) - 32 ounces,
         (910 grams, 2,105 yards)
      Color B (Rose) - 9½ ounces,
         (270 grams, 625 yards)
      Color C (Green) - 26 ounces,
         (740 grams, 1,710 yards)
   Crochet hook, size K (6.50 mm) **or** size needed for
      gauge

GAUGE: 15 dc and 7 rows = 4″
          One Strip = 4¼″ wide

SHELL
(2 Dc, ch 2, 2 dc) in stitch or space indicated.

STRIP (Make 12)
Note: Strip will be longer than finished length before
Stripe is worked.

CENTER
With Color A, ch 15 **loosely**.
Row 1 (Right side): Dc in fourth ch from hook and in
next ch, skip next 3 chs, work Shell in next ch, skip
next 3 chs, dc in last 3 chs: 12 sts.
Note: Loop a short piece of yarn around Shell to mark
last row as **right** side and bottom edge.
Rows 2-133: Ch 3 **(counts as first dc, now and
throughout)**, turn; dc in next 2 dc, work Shell in next
Shell (ch-2 sp), dc in last 3 sts: 10 dc.
Finish off.

EDGING
FIRST SIDE
With **right** side facing and working in end of rows, join
Color C with slip st in first row; ch 3, 4 dc in same row,
★ working **in front** of first 2 dc on next row, work FPtr
around post of third dc **(Fig. 13d, page 138)**, 5 dc in
next row; repeat from ★ across; finish off: 401 sts.

SECOND SIDE
Work same as First Side.

STRIPE
FIRST LINE
With **right** side facing and beginning at bottom edge,
join Color B with slip st around first 3 chs skipped on
beginning ch of Center; ★ working vertically, sc
loosely in sp **between** third dc and Shell on next row;
repeat from ★ to end; finish off.

SECOND LINE
With **right** side facing and beginning at bottom edge,
join Color B with slip st around second 3 chs skipped
on beginning ch of Center; ★ working vertically, sc
loosely in sp **between** Shell and next dc on next row;
repeat from ★ to end; finish off.

JOINING
With **wrong** sides of two Strips together, **bottom**
edges at the same end and working through both
pieces, join Color B with slip st in center dc of first 5-dc
group; ch 1, sc in same st, ★ ch 3, sc in center dc of next
5-dc group; repeat from ★ across; finish off.
Join remaining Strips in same manner.

BORDER

TOP

With **right** side of short end facing, join Color C with slip st in last dc of Edging; 5 tr **between** next 2 dc of same Strip, work FPtr around last sc of First Stripe Line, 5 tr in next Shell, work FPtr around last sc of Second Stripe Line, 5 tr **between** next 2 dc on same Strip, work FPtr around last ch-3 of Joining; ★ † working across next Strip, 5 tr **between** next 2 dc, work FPtr around last sc of First Stripe Line, 5 tr in next Shell, work FPtr around last sc of Second Stripe Line, 5 tr **between** next 2 dc on same Strip †, work FPtr around last ch-3 of Joining; repeat from ★ across to last Strip, then repeat from † to † once, slip st in first dc of Edging; finish off.

BOTTOM

With **right** side of short end facing, join Color C with slip st in last dc of Edging; working over beginning ch on **each** Strip, 5 tr **between** next 2 dc of same Strip, work FPtr around first sc of Second Stripe Line, 5 tr in next Shell (center of Shell), work FPtr around first sc of First Stripe Line, 5 tr **between** next 2 dc on same Strip, work FPtr around first ch-3 of Joining; ★ † working across next Strip, 5 tr **between** next 2 dc, work FPtr around first sc of Second Stripe Line, 5 tr in next Shell (center of Shell), work FPtr around first sc of First Stripe Line, 5 tr **between** next 2 dc on same Strip †, work FPtr around first ch-3 of Joining; repeat from ★ across to last Strip, then repeat from † to † once, slip st in first dc of Edging; finish off.

TANTALIZINGLY TEAL

This tantalizingly teal afghan makes a nice fireside companion. Fashioned holding two strands of yarn together as you crochet, it features a pretty block look that's quick and easy to make.

Finished Size: Approximately 48″ x 69″

MATERIALS

Worsted Weight Yarn, approximately:
76 ounces, (2,160 grams, 4,835 yards)
Crochet hook, size Q (15.00 mm) **or** size needed for gauge

GAUGE: In pattern, (sc, 3 dc) 3 times and 3 rows = 6″

Note: Entire afghan is worked holding two strands of yarn together.

Ch 76 **loosely.**
Row 1: 2 Dc in fourth ch from hook, skip next 2 chs, ★ (sc, 3 dc) in next ch, skip next 2 chs; repeat from ★ across to last ch, sc in last ch: 96 sts.
Row 2 (Right side): Ch 3 **(counts as first dc, now and throughout)**, turn; 2 dc in same st, ★ skip next 3 dc, (sc, 3 dc) in next sc; repeat from ★ across to last 3 sts, skip next 2 dc, sc in top of beginning ch.
Note: Loop a short piece of yarn around any stitch to mark last row as **right** side.
Row 3: Ch 3, turn; 2 dc in same st, ★ skip next 3 dc, (sc, 3 dc) in next sc; repeat from ★ across to last 3 dc, skip next 2 dc, sc in last dc.
Repeat Row 3 until afghan measures approximately 681/2″, ending by working a **right** side row; do **not** finish off.
Last Row: Ch 1, turn; sc in first sc, ch 2, (skip next 3 dc, sc in next sc, ch 2) across to last 3 dc, skip next 2 dc, sc in last dc; finish off.

Add fringe **(Figs. 25a & b, page 142)**.

FIRESIDE CHEER

*Venturing outdoors in the wintertime will be even more fun when you have
this warm throw for snuggling by the fire when you return. Fashioned
with a Fair Isle look, it captures all the cheerfulness of the season.*

Finished Size: Approximately 43" x 58"

MATERIALS

Worsted Weight Yarn, approximately:
Main Color (Ecru) - 23 ounces,
(650 grams, 1,515 yards)
Color A (Blue) - 10 ounces, (280 grams, 660 yards)
Color B (Red) - 8 ounces, (230 grams, 525 yards)
Crochet hook, size H (5.00 mm) **or** size needed for
gauge

GAUGE: 14 sc and 16 rows = 4"

With Color A, ch 152 **loosely**.

Row 1: Sc in second ch from hook and in each ch
across, changing to Color B in last sc *(Fig. 21,
page 141)*: 151 sc.

Row 2 (Right side): Ch 1, turn; sc in each sc across,
changing to MC in last sc.

Note: Loop a short piece of yarn around any stitch to
mark last row as **right** side.

Row 3: Ch 1, turn; sc in first sc, (ch 1, skip next sc,
sc in next sc) across, changing to Color B in last sc:
75 ch-1 sps.

Row 4: Ch 1, turn; sc in first sc; working in **front** of
ch-1, (dc in sc one row **below** next ch-1, sc in next sc)
across, changing to Color A in last sc.

Row 5: Ch 1, turn; sc in each st across, changing to MC
in last sc.

Row 6: Ch 1, turn; sc in each sc across, changing to
Color B in last sc.

Row 7: Ch 1, turn; sc in first 2 sts, ch 1, skip next sc, sc
in next sc, ch 1, ★ skip next sc, sc in next 3 sts, ch 1, skip
next sc, sc in next sc, ch 1; repeat from ★ across to last
3 sts, skip next sc, sc in last 2 sts, changing to MC in last
sc.

Row 8: Ch 1, turn; sc in first 2 sc; working in **front** of
next ch-1, dc in sc one row **below** ch-1, sc in next sc;
working in **front** of next ch-1, dc in sc one row **below**
ch-1, ★ sc in next 3 sc; working in **front** of next ch-1, dc
in sc one row **below** ch-1, sc in next sc; working in
front of next ch-1, dc in sc one row **below** ch-1; repeat
from ★ across to last 2 sc, sc in last 2 sc, changing to
Color A in last sc.

Row 9: Ch 1, turn; sc in first sc, ★ ch 1, skip next sc, sc
in next 3 sts, ch 1, skip next sc, sc in next sc; repeat

from ★ across, changing to MC in last sc.

Row 10: Ch 1, turn; sc in first sc, ★ working in **front** of
next ch-1, dc in sc one row **below** ch-1, ch 1, skip next
sc, sc in next sc, ch 1, skip next sc; working in **front** of
next ch-1, dc in sc one row **below** ch-1, sc in next sc;
repeat from ★ across, changing to Color A in last sc.

Row 11: Ch 1, turn; sc in first sc, ★ ch 1, skip next dc;
working in **back** of next ch-1, dc in sc one row **below**
ch-1, sc in next sc; working in **back** of next ch-1, dc in sc
one row **below** ch-1, ch 1, skip next dc, sc in next sc;
repeat from ★ across, changing to MC in last sc.

Row 12: Ch 1, turn; sc in first sc, ★ working in **front** of
next ch-1, dc in dc one row **below** ch-1, sc in next 3 sts;
working in **front** of next ch-1, dc in dc one row **below**
ch-1, sc in next sc; repeat from ★ across, changing to
Color B in last sc.

Rows 13 and 14: Repeat Rows 7 and 8.

Row 15: Ch 1, turn; sc in each st across, changing to
Color B in last sc.

Rows 16-33: Repeat Rows 2-15 once; then repeat
Rows 2-5 once **more**.

Row 34: Ch 1, turn; sc in each sc across, changing to
Color A in last sc.

Row 35: Ch 1, turn; sc in first 2 sts, ch 3, ★ skip next
3 sts, sc in next st, ch 3; repeat from ★ across to last
5 sts, skip next 3 sts, sc in last 2 sts, changing to MC in
last sc.

Row 36: Ch 1, turn; sc in first 2 sc; working in **front** of
next ch-3, (dc in **next** st one row **below** ch-3) 3 times,
★ sc in next st; working in **front** of next ch-3, (dc in **next**
st one row **below** ch-3) 3 times; repeat from ★ across to
last 2 sc, sc in last 2 sc, changing to Color A in last sc.

Row 37: Ch 1, turn; sc in first sc, ch 2, skip next 2 sts,
sc in next dc, ★ ch 3, skip next 3 sts, sc in next dc; repeat
from ★ across to last 3 sts, ch 2, skip next 2 sts, sc in last
sc, changing to MC.

Row 38: Ch 1, turn; sc in first sc; working in **front** of
next ch-2, (dc in **next** st one row **below** ch-2) twice, sc
in next sc; ★ working in **front** of next ch-3, (dc in **next** st
one row **below** ch-3) 3 times, sc in next sc; repeat from
★ across to last ch-2; working in **front** of last ch-2, (dc in
next st one row **below** ch-2) twice, sc in last sc,
changing to Color A.

Rows 39-43: Repeat Rows 35-38 once; then repeat
Row 35 once **more**.

Row 44: Ch 1, turn; sc in first 2 sc; working in **front** of

106

next ch-3, (dc in **next** st one row **below** ch-3) 3 times, ★ sc in next sc; working in **front** of next ch-3, (dc in **next** st one row **below** ch-3) 3 times; repeat from ★ across to last 2 sc, sc in last 2 sc, changing to Color B in last sc.

Row 45: Ch 1, turn; sc in first sc, ch 2, skip next 2 sts, sc in next st, ★ ch 3, skip next 3 sts, sc in next st; repeat from ★ across to last 3 sts, ch 2, skip next 2 sts, sc in last sc, changing to MC.

Row 46: Ch 1, turn; sc in first sc; working in **front** of next ch-2, (dc in **next** st one row **below** ch-2) twice, sc in next sc, ★ working in **front** of next ch-3, (dc in **next** st one row **below** ch-3) 3 times, sc in next sc; repeat from ★ across to last ch-2; working in **front** of last ch-2, (dc in **next** st one row **below** ch-2) twice, sc in last sc, changing to Color B.

Row 47: Ch 1, turn; sc in first sc, ch 1, ★ skip next dc, sc in next 3 sts, ch 1; repeat from ★ across to last 2 sts, skip next dc, sc in last sc, changing to MC.

Row 48: Ch 1, turn; sc in first sc; working in **front** of next ch-1, dc in dc one row **below** ch-1, ★ sc in next 3 sc; working in **front** of next ch-1, dc in dc one row **below** ch-1; repeat from ★ across to last sc, sc in last sc, changing to Color B.

Row 49: Repeat Row 45.

Row 50: Ch 1, turn; sc in first sc; working in **front** of next ch-2, (dc in **next** st one row **below** ch-2) twice, sc in next sc, ★ working in **front** of next ch-3, (dc in **next** st one row **below** ch-3) 3 times, sc in next sc; repeat from ★ across to last ch-2; working in **front** of last ch-2, (dc in **next** st one row **below** ch-2) twice, sc in last sc, changing to Color A.

Rows 51-60: Repeat Rows 35-38 twice; then repeat Rows 35 and 36 once **more**.

Row 61: Ch 1, turn; sc in each st across, changing to Color B in last sc.

Rows 62-199: Repeat Rows 16-61, 3 times.

Rows 200-231: Repeat Rows 2-33; do **not** finish off.

EDGING

Ch 3, turn; dc evenly around, working 3 dc in each corner; join with slip st to top of beginning ch-3, finish off.

CANDY STRIPES

Peppermint stripes and double ruffles make this afghan and pillow set perfect for Christmas.

MATERIALS
Sport Weight Yarn, approximately:
Afghan
    MC (White) - 35 ounces, (990 grams, 3,365 yards)
    CC (Red) - 16 ounces, (460 grams, 1,495 yards)
Pillow
    MC (White) - 4 ounces, (110 grams, 375 yards)
    CC (Red) - 2 ounces, (60 grams, 190 yards)
Crochet hook, size F (3.75 mm) **or** size needed for gauge
Polyester stuffing

GAUGE: In pattern, 16 sc and 20 rows = 4"

AFGHAN

Finished Size: Approximately 42" x 58"

With MC, ch 221 **loosely**.
Row 1 (Right side): Sc in second ch from hook and in each ch across: 220 sc.

Note: Loop a short piece of yarn around any stitch to mark last row as **right** side.

Row 2: Ch 1, turn; sc in each sc across.

Row 3: Ch 1, turn; working in Back Loops Only *(Fig. 18, page 140)*, sc in each sc across.

Rows 4 and 5: Ch 1, turn; working in **both** loops, sc in each sc across; at end of Row 5, drop MC, do **not** finish off.

Note: Stripes create a double thickness.

Stripe - Row 1: With **right** side facing and working in free loops 3 rows below *(Fig. 19a, page 140)*, join CC with slip st in first st; ch 1, sc in same st and in each st across.

Stripe - Rows 2 and 3: Ch 1, turn; working in **both** loops, sc in each sc across; at end of Row 3 finish off.

Row 6 (Joining): With **wrong** side facing, pick up MC, ch 1; working in **both** loops of last MC **and** CC rows, sc in each st across.

Rows 7 and 8: Ch 1, turn; sc in each sc across.

Rows 9-194: Repeat Rows 3-8, 31 times; do **not** finish off.

FIRST EDGING

Rnd 1: Ch 1, do **not** turn; working in end of rows, sc in each row across; working in free loops of beginning ch *(Fig. 19b, page 140)*, 3 sc in first ch, sc in each ch across to last ch, 3 sc in last ch; working in end of rows, sc in each row across; 3 sc in first sc, sc in each sc across to last sc, 3 sc in last sc; join with slip to first sc: 836 sc.

Rnd 2: Ch 1, working in Front Loops Only, sc in each sc around, working 3 sc in each corner sc; join with slip st to first sc: 844 sc.

Rnds 3 and 4: Ch 1, working in **both** loops, sc in each sc around, working 3 sc in each corner sc; join with slip st to first sc: 860 sc.

Rnd 5: Ch 1, sc in same st, skip next sc, 5 dc in next sc, skip next sc, ★ sc in next sc, skip next sc, 5 dc in next sc, skip next sc; repeat from ★ around; join with slip st to first sc, finish off.

SECOND EDGING

Note: When working in stitch adjacent to end of Stripe Row, work in free loop and end of Stripe Row at the same time.

Rnd 1: With **right** side facing and working in free loops of Rnd 1 on First Edging *(Fig. 19a, page 140)*, join CC with slip st in any corner sc; ch 1, 3 sc in same st, sc in each sc around, working 3 sc in each corner sc; join with slip st to first sc: 844 sc.

Rnd 2: Ch 1, sc in same st, skip next sc, 5 dc in next sc, skip next sc, ★ sc in next sc, skip next sc, 5 dc in next sc, skip next sc; repeat from ★ around; join with slip st to first sc, finish off.

PILLOW

Finished Size: Approximately 12″ x 12½″

FRONT

With MC, ch 39 **loosely**.

Row 1 (Right side): Sc in second ch from hook and in each ch across: 38 sc.

Note: Loop a short piece of yarn around any stitch to mark last row as **right** side.

Row 2: Ch 1, turn; sc in each sc across.

Row 3: Ch 1, turn; working in Back Loops Only *(Fig. 18, page 140)*, sc in each sc across.

Rows 4 and 5: Ch 1, turn; working in **both** loops, sc in each sc across; at end of Row 5, drop MC, do **not** finish off.

Note: Stripes create a double thickness.

Stripe - Row 1: With **right** side facing and working in free loops 3 rows below, join CC with slip st in first st; ch 1, sc in same st and in each st across.

Stripe - Rows 2 and 3: Ch 1, turn; working in **both** loops, sc in each sc across; at end of Row 3 finish off.

Row 6 (Joining): With **wrong** side facing, pick up MC, ch 1; working in **both** loops of last MC **and** CC rows, sc in each st across.

Rows 7 and 8: Ch 1, turn; sc in each sc across.

Rows 9-50: Repeat Rows 3-8, 7 times.

Finish off.

BACK

Work same as Front; do **not** finish off.

FIRST EDGING

Rnd 1: Ch 1, turn; holding both pieces with **wrong** sides together, Back facing and working through **both** pieces, 3 sc in first sc, sc in each sc across to last sc, 3 sc in last sc; working in end of rows, sc in each row across; working in free loops of beginning ch *(Fig. 19b, page 140)*, 3 sc in first ch, sc in each ch across to last ch, 3 sc in last ch; add stuffing, working in end of rows, sc in each row across; join with slip st to first sc: 184 sc.

Rnd 2: Ch 1, working in Front Loops Only, sc in each sc around, working 3 sc in each corner sc; join with slip st to first sc: 192 sc.

Rnds 3 and 4: Ch 1, working in **both** loops, sc in each sc around, working 3 sc in each corner sc; join with slip st to first sc: 200 sc.

Rnd 5: Ch 1, sc in same st, skip next sc, 5 dc in next sc, skip next sc, ★ sc in next sc, skip next sc, 5 dc in next sc, skip next sc; repeat from ★ around; join with slip st to first sc, finish off.

SECOND EDGING

Note: When working in stitch adjacent to end of Stripe Row, work in free loop and end of Stripe Row at the same time.

Rnd 1: With Front facing and working in free loops of Rnd 1 on First Edging *(Fig. 19a, page 140)*, join CC with slip st in any corner sc; ch 1, 3 sc in same st, sc in each sc around, working 3 sc in each corner sc; join with slip st to first sc: 192 sc.

Rnd 2: Ch 1, sc in same st, skip next sc, 5 dc in next sc, skip next sc, ★ sc in next sc, skip next sc, 5 dc in next sc, skip next sc; repeat from ★ around; join with slip st to first sc, finish off.

VALENTINE AFGHAN

*On Valentine's Day, this luscious raspberry afghan will tempt
your loved one to stay home and cuddle. Featuring a trio of hearts
fashioned with popcorn stitches, it sets a sentimental mood.*

Finished Size: Approximately 55" x 67"

MATERIALS
Worsted Weight Yarn, approximately:
  49 ounces, (1,400 grams, 3,220 yards)
Crochet hook, size G (4.00 mm) **or** size needed for
  gauge

GAUGE: In pattern, 16 sts and 8 rows = 4"

PATTERN STITCHES
POPCORN (abbreviated PC)
Work 5 dc in next st, drop loop from hook, insert hook
in first dc of 5-dc group, hook dropped loop and draw
through, pushing PC to **right** side *(Fig. 12, page 137)*,
ch 1 to close.
PANEL
Dc in next 6 dc, work PC, dc in next 5 dc, work PC,
dc in next 6 dc.

Ch 221 **loosely**.
Row 1 (Right side): Dc in eighth ch from hook, (ch 2,
skip next 2 chs, dc in next ch) across: 72 sps.

Row 2: Ch 5, turn; dc in next dc, dc in each ch and in
each dc across to last sp, ch 2, skip next 2 chs, dc in
next ch.
Row 3: Ch 5, turn; dc in next dc and in each st across to
last sp, ch 2, skip next 2 chs, dc in next ch.
Row 4: Ch 5, turn; dc in next 6 dc, work PC, (dc in
next 5 dc, work PC) 33 times, dc in next 6 dc, ch 2,
skip next 2 chs, dc in next ch: 34 PC.
Row 5: Ch 5, turn; dc in next dc and in each st across to
last sp, ch 2, skip next 2 chs, dc in next ch.
Row 6: Ch 5, turn; dc in next 6 dc, work PC, dc in each
dc across to last 7 dc, work PC, dc in next 6 dc, ch 2,
skip next 2 chs, dc in next ch.
Row 7: Repeat Row 5.
Rows 8 and 9: Repeat Rows 4 and 5.
Row 10: Ch 5, turn; dc in next 6 dc, work PC, dc in
next 5 dc, work PC, dc in each dc across to last 13 dc,
work PC, dc in next 5 dc, work PC, dc in next 6 dc,
ch 2, skip next 2 chs, dc in next ch.
Row 11: Ch 5, turn; dc in next 19 sts, ch 2, (skip next
2 dc, dc in next dc, ch 2) across to last 21 sts, skip next
2 dc, dc in next 19 sts, ch 2, skip next 2 chs, dc in next
ch: 60 sps.
Row 12: Ch 5, turn; work Panel, ch 2, (dc in next dc,
ch 2) 57 times, work Panel, ch 2, skip next 2 chs, dc in
next ch.
Row 13: Ch 5, turn; dc in next 19 sts, (ch 2, dc in next
dc) twice, (dc in next 2 chs and in next dc) 54 times,
ch 2, dc in next dc, ch 2, dc in next 19 sts, ch 2, skip next
2 chs, dc in next ch.
Row 14: Ch 5, turn; work Panel, ch 2, dc in next dc,
ch 2, dc in each dc across to next ch-2 sp, ch 2, dc in
next dc, ch 2, work Panel, ch 2, skip next 2 chs, dc in
next ch.
Row 15: Ch 5, turn; dc in next 19 sts, ch 2, dc in next
dc, ch 2, dc in each st across to next ch-2 sp, ch 2, dc in
next dc, ch 2, dc in next 19 sts, ch 2, skip next 2 chs,
dc in next ch.
Row 16: Ch 5, turn; work Panel, ch 2, dc in next dc,
ch 2, dc in next 6 dc, work PC, (dc in next 5 dc, work
PC) 25 times, dc in next 6 dc, ch 2, dc in next dc, ch 2,
work Panel, ch 2, skip next 2 chs, dc in next ch: 30 PC.
Row 17: Repeat Row 15.
Row 18: Ch 5, turn; work Panel, ch 2, dc in next dc,
ch 2, dc in next 6 dc, work PC, dc in next 149 dc, work
PC, dc in next 6 dc, ch 2, dc in next dc, ch 2, work

Panel, ch 2, skip next 2 chs, dc in next ch.

Rows 19-21: Repeat Rows 15 and 16 once, then repeat Row 15 once **more**.

Row 22: Ch 5, turn; work Panel, ch 2, dc in next dc, ch 2, dc in next 6 dc, work PC, dc in next 5 dc, work PC, dc in next 137 dc, work PC, dc in next 5 dc, work PC, dc in next 6 dc, ch 2, dc in next dc, ch 2, work Panel, ch 2, skip next 2 chs, dc in next ch.

Row 23: Repeat Row 15.

Row 24: Ch 5, turn; work Panel, ch 2, dc in next dc, ch 2, work Panel, ch 2, (skip next 2 dc, dc in next dc, ch 2) 41 times, skip next 2 dc, work Panel, ch 2, dc in next dc, ch 2, work Panel, ch 2, skip next 2 chs, dc in next ch: 48 sps.

Row 25: Ch 5, turn; † dc in next 19 sts, ch 2, dc in next dc, ch 2, dc in next 19 sts, ch 2 †, (dc in next dc, ch 2) 41 times, repeat from † to † once, skip next 2 chs, dc in next ch.

Row 26: Ch 5, turn; (work Panel, ch 2, dc in next dc, ch 2) twice, dc in next dc, (dc in next 2 chs and in next dc) 38 times, (ch 2, dc in next dc, ch 2, work Panel) twice, ch 2, skip next 2 chs, dc in next ch.

Row 27: Ch 5, turn; (dc in next 19 sts, ch 2, dc in next dc, ch 2) twice, dc in next 115 sts, (ch 2, dc in next dc, ch 2, dc in next 19 sts) twice, ch 2, skip next 2 chs, dc in next ch.

Row 28: Ch 5, turn; (work Panel, ch 2, dc in next dc, ch 2) twice, dc in next 6 dc, work PC, (dc in next 5 dc, work PC) 17 times, dc in next 6 dc, (ch 2, dc in next dc, ch 2, work Panel) twice, ch 2, skip next 2 chs, dc in next ch: 26 PC.

Row 29: Repeat Row 27.

Row 30: Ch 5, turn; (work Panel, ch 2, dc in next dc, ch 2) twice, dc in next 6 dc, work PC, dc in next 101 dc, work PC, dc in next 6 dc, (ch 2, dc in next dc, ch 2, work Panel) twice, ch 2, skip next 2 chs, dc in next ch: 10 PC.

Rows 31-33: Repeat Rows 27 and 28 once, then repeat Row 27 once **more**.

Row 34: Ch 5, turn; (work Panel, ch 2, dc in next dc, ch 2) twice, dc in next 6 dc, work PC, dc in next 5 dc, work PC, dc in next 89 dc, work PC, dc in next 5 dc, work PC, dc in next 6 dc, (ch 2, dc in next dc, ch 2, work Panel) twice, ch 2, skip next 2 chs, dc in next ch: 12 PC.

Row 35: Ch 5, turn; † (dc in next 19 sts, ch 2, dc in next dc, ch 2) twice, dc in next 19 sts, ch 2 †, (skip next 2 dc, dc in next dc, ch 2) 25 times, skip next 2 dc, repeat from † to † once, skip next 2 chs, dc in next ch: 36 sps.

Row 36: Ch 5, turn; (work Panel, ch 2, dc in next dc, ch 2) 3 times, (dc in next dc, ch 2) 24 times, work Panel, (ch 2, dc in next dc, ch 2, work Panel) twice, ch 2, skip next 2 chs, dc in next ch: 12 PC.

Row 37: Ch 5, turn; (dc in next 19 sts, ch 2, dc in next dc, ch 2) 3 times, dc in next dc, (dc in next 2 chs and in next dc) 22 times, (ch 2, dc in next dc, ch 2, dc in next 19 sts) 3 times, ch 2, skip next 2 chs, dc in next ch: 14 sps.

Row 38: Ch 5, turn; (work Panel, ch 2, dc in next dc, ch 2) 3 times, dc in next 67 dc, (ch 2, dc in next dc, ch 2, work Panel) 3 times, ch 2, skip next 2 chs, dc in next ch.

Row 39: Ch 5, turn; (dc in next 19 sts, ch 2, dc in next dc, ch 2) 3 times, dc in next 67 sts, (ch 2, dc in next dc, ch 2, dc in next 19 sts) 3 times, ch 2, skip next 2 chs, dc in next ch.

Row 40: Ch 5, turn; (work Panel, ch 2, dc in next dc, ch 2) 3 times, dc in next 6 dc, work PC, (dc in next 5 dc, work PC) 9 times, dc in next 6 dc, (ch 2, dc in next dc, ch 2, work Panel) 3 times, ch 2, skip next 2 chs, dc in next ch: 22 PC.

Row 41: Repeat Row 39.

Row 42: Ch 5, turn; (work Panel, ch 2, dc in next dc, ch 2) 3 times, dc in next 6 dc, work PC, dc in next 53 sts, work PC, dc in next 6 dc, (ch 2, dc in next dc, ch 2, work Panel) 3 times, ch 2, skip next 2 chs, dc in next ch: 14 PC.

Row 43: Repeat Row 39.

Row 44: Repeat Row 42.

Row 45: Ch 5, turn; (dc in next 19 sts, ch 2, dc in next dc, ch 2) 3 times, dc in next 35 sts, (work PC, dc in next dc) twice, work PC, dc in next 27 sts, (ch 2, dc in next dc, ch 2, dc in next 19 sts) 3 times, ch 2, skip next 2 chs, dc in next ch.

Row 46: Ch 5, turn; (work Panel, ch 2, dc in next dc, ch 2) 3 times, dc in next 6 dc, work PC, dc in next 18 sts, work PC, dc in next 7 sts, work PC, dc in next 26 sts, work PC, dc in next 6 dc, (ch 2, dc in next dc, ch 2, work Panel) 3 times, ch 2, skip next 2 chs, dc in next ch: 16 PC.

Row 47: Ch 5, turn; (dc in next 19 sts, ch 2, dc in next dc, ch 2) 3 times, dc in next 31 sts, work PC, dc in next 11 sts, work PC, dc in next 23 sts, (ch 2, dc in next dc, ch 2, dc in next 19 sts) 3 times, ch 2, skip next 2 chs, dc in next ch.

Row 48: Ch 5, turn; (work Panel, ch 2, dc in next dc, ch 2) 3 times, dc in next 6 dc, work PC, dc in next 16 sts, work PC, dc in next 13 sts, work PC, dc in next 22 sts, work PC, dc in next 6 dc, (ch 2, dc in next dc, ch 2, work Panel) 3 times, ch 2, skip next 2 chs, dc in next ch: 16 PC.

Row 49: Ch 5, turn; (dc in next 19 sts, ch 2, dc in next dc, ch 2) 3 times, dc in next 27 sts, work PC, dc in next 15 sts, work PC, dc in next 23 sts, (ch 2, dc in next dc, ch 2, dc in next 19 sts) 3 times, ch 2, skip next 2 chs, dc in next ch.

Row 50: Ch 5, turn; (work Panel, ch 2, dc in next dc, ch 2) 3 times, dc in next 6 dc, work PC, dc in next 18 sts, work PC, dc in next 15 sts, work PC, dc in next 18 sts, work PC, dc in next 6 dc, (ch 2, dc in next dc, ch 2, work Panel) 3 times, ch 2, skip next 2 chs, dc in

next ch: 16 PC.

Row 51: Ch 5, turn; (dc in next 19 sts, ch 2, dc in next dc, ch 2) 3 times, dc in next 23 sts, work PC, dc in next 15 sts, work PC, dc in next 27 sts, (ch 2, dc in next dc, ch 2, dc in next 19 sts) 3 times, ch 2, skip next 2 chs, dc in next ch.

Row 52: Repeat Row 50.
Row 53: Repeat Row 49.
Row 54: Repeat Row 48.
Row 55: Repeat Row 47.
Row 56: Repeat Row 46.
Row 57: Repeat Row 45.
Rows 58-60: Repeat Rows 42-44.

Row 61: Ch 5, turn; (dc in next 19 sts, ch 2, dc in next dc, ch 2) 3 times, dc in next 27 sts, (work PC, dc in next dc) twice, work PC, dc in next 35 sts, (ch 2, dc in next dc, ch 2, dc in next 19 sts) 3 times, ch 2, skip next 2 chs, dc in next ch.

Row 62: Ch 5, turn; (work Panel, ch 2, dc in next dc, ch 2) 3 times, dc in next 6 dc, work PC, dc in next 26 sts, work PC, dc in next 7 sts, work PC, dc in next 18 sts, work PC, dc in next 6 dc, (ch 2, dc in next dc, ch 2, work Panel) 3 times, ch 2, skip next 2 chs, dc in next ch: 16 PC.

Row 63: Ch 5, turn; (dc in next 19 sts, ch 2, dc in next dc, ch 2) 3 times, dc in next 23 sts, work PC, dc in next 11 sts, work PC, dc in next 31 sts, (ch 2, dc in next dc, ch 2, dc in next 19 sts) 3 times, ch 2, skip next 2 chs, dc in next ch.

Row 64: Ch 5, turn; (work Panel, ch 2, dc in next dc, ch 2) 3 times, dc in next 6 dc, work PC, dc in next 22 sts, work PC, dc in next 13 sts, work PC, dc in next 16 sts, work PC, dc in next 6 dc, (ch 2, dc in next dc, ch 2, work Panel) 3 times, ch 2, skip next 2 chs, dc in next ch: 16 PC.

Row 65: Ch 5, turn; (dc in next 19 sts, ch 2, dc in next dc, ch 2) 3 times, dc in next 23 sts, work PC, dc in next 15 sts, work PC, dc in next 27 sts, (ch 2, dc in next dc, ch 2, dc in next 19 sts) 3 times, ch 2, skip next 2 chs, dc in next ch.

Row 66: Repeat Row 50.
Row 67: Repeat Row 49.
Row 68: Repeat Row 50.
Row 69: Repeat Row 65.
Row 70: Repeat Row 64.
Row 71: Repeat Row 63.
Row 72: Repeat Row 62.
Row 73: Repeat Row 61.
Rows 74-92: Repeat Rows 42-60.
Rows 93-95: Repeat Rows 39 and 40 once, then repeat Row 39 once **more**.
Rows 96 and 97: Repeat Rows 38 and 39.
Row 98: Ch 5, turn; (work Panel, ch 2, dc in next dc, ch 2) 3 times, dc in next dc, (ch 2, skip next 2 dc, dc in next dc) 22 times, (ch 2, dc in next dc, ch 2, work Panel)

3 times, ch 2, skip next 2 chs, dc in next ch.

Row 99: Ch 5, turn; † (dc in next 19 sts, ch 2, dc in next dc, ch 2) twice, dc in next 19 sts, ch 2 †, (dc in next dc, ch 2) 25 times, repeat from † to † once, skip next 2 chs, dc in next ch.

Row 100: Ch 5, turn; † (work Panel, ch 2, dc in next dc, ch 2) twice, work Panel †, dc in next 2 chs, (dc in next dc and in next 2 chs) 25 times, repeat from † to † once, ch 2, skip next 2 chs, dc in next ch.

Rows 101-107: Repeat Rows 27-33.

Row 108: Ch 5, turn; (work Panel, ch 2, dc in next dc, ch 2) twice, dc in next 115 sts, (ch 2, dc in next dc, ch 2, work Panel) twice, ch 2, skip next 2 chs, dc in next ch.

Row 109: Ch 5, turn; (dc in next 19 sts, ch 2, dc in next dc, ch 2) twice, dc in next dc, ch 2, (skip next 2 dc, dc in next dc, ch 2) 38 times, (dc in next dc, ch 2, dc in next 19 sts, ch 2) twice, skip next 2 chs, dc in next ch: 48 sps.

Row 110: Ch 5, turn; † work Panel, ch 2, dc in next dc, ch 2, work Panel, ch 2 †, (dc in next dc, ch 2) 41 times, repeat from † to † once, skip next 2 chs, dc in next ch.

Row 111: Ch 5, turn; † dc in next 19 sts, ch 2, dc in next dc, ch 2, dc in next 19 sts †, dc in next 2 chs, (dc in next dc and in next 2 chs) 41 times, repeat from † to † once, ch 2, skip next 2 chs, dc in next ch.

Row 112: Repeat Row 22.
Rows 113-119: Repeat Rows 15-21.
Rows 120 and 121: Repeat Rows 14 and 15.
Row 122: Ch 5, turn; work Panel, ch 2, (dc in next dc, ch 2) twice, (skip next 2 dc, dc in next dc, ch 2) 54 times, dc in next dc, ch 2, work Panel, ch 2, skip next 2 chs, dc in next ch: 60 sps.

Row 123: Ch 5, turn; dc in next 19 sts, ch 2, (dc in next dc, ch 2) across to Panel, dc in next 19 sts, ch 2, skip next 2 chs, dc in next ch.

Row 124: Ch 5, turn; work Panel, dc in next 2 chs, (dc in next dc and in next 2 chs) 57 times, work Panel, ch 2, skip next 2 chs, dc in next ch.

Row 125: Repeat Row 5.
Rows 126-128: Repeat Rows 4-6.
Row 129: Repeat Row 5.
Row 130: Repeat Row 4.
Rows 131 and 132: Repeat Row 3, twice.
Row 133: Ch 5, turn; dc in next dc, ch 2, (skip next 2 dc, dc in next dc, ch 2) across to last sp, skip next 2 chs, dc in next ch; do **not** finish off.

EDGING

Ch 1, do **not** turn; sc evenly around, working 3 sc in corners; join with slip st to first sc, finish off.

CHRISTMAS TREES

The Yuletide season wouldn't be complete without the traditional evergreen tree. To honor this familiar symbol of the holidays, we used cluster stitches to bring added dimension to the tree motifs.

Finished Size: Approximately 42 x 63"

MATERIALS

Worsted Weight Yarn, approximately:
Main Color (Ecru) -24½ ounces,
(700 grams, 1,645 yards)
Color A (Red) - 14½ ounces,
(410 grams, 975 yards)
Color B (Green) - 8½ ounces,
(240 grams, 570 yards)
Crochet hook, size J (6.00 mm) **or** size needed for gauge
Bobbins
Yarn needle

GAUGE: One Square = 7" x 7"

CLUSTER

★ YO, insert hook in stitch indicated, YO and pull up a loop, YO and draw through 2 loops on hook; repeat from ★ 2 times **more**, YO and draw through all 4 loops on hook *(Figs. 9a & b, page 135)*.

USING BOBBINS

Wind small amounts of each color onto a bobbin to keep the different color yarns from tangling. You'll need one bobbin for each color change. Always keep the bobbins on the **wrong** side.

To change colors, work last stitch before color change to last step, hook new yarn and draw through both loops on hook *(Fig. 21, page 141)*; do **not** cut yarn.

SQUARE (Make 54)

With MC, ch 16 **loosely**.

Row 1 (Right side): Sc in second ch from hook and in each ch across: 15 sc.

Note: Loop a short piece of yarn around any stitch to mark last row as **right** side.

Row 2: Ch 2 **(counts as first hdc, now and throughout)**, turn; dc in next sc, (sc in next sc, dc in next sc) twice, with Color B sc in next sc, work Cluster in next sc, sc in next sc, with MC dc in next sc, (sc in next sc, dc in next sc) twice, hdc in last sc.

Row 3: Ch 1, turn; sc in first 5 sts, with Color B sc in next 4 sts, with MC sc in last 6 sts.

Row 4: Ch 2, turn; dc in next sc, with Color B sc in next sc, (work Cluster in next sc, sc in next sc) 5 times, with MC dc in next sc, hdc in last sc.

Row 5: Ch 1, turn; sc in first 2 sts, with Color B sc in next 10 sts, with MC sc in last 3 sts.

Row 6: Ch 2, turn; sc in next sc, dc in next sc, with Color B sc in next sc, (work Cluster in next sc, sc in next sc) 4 times, with MC dc in next sc, sc in next sc, hdc in last sc.

Row 7: Ch 1, turn; sc in first 3 sts, with Color B sc in next 8 sts, with MC sc in last 4 sts.

Row 8: Ch 2, turn; dc in next sc, sc in next sc, dc in next sc, with Color B sc in next sc, (work Cluster in next sc, sc in next sc) 3 times, with MC dc in next sc, sc in next sc, dc in next sc, hdc in last sc.

Row 9: Ch 1, turn; sc in first 4 sts, with Color B sc in next 6 sts, with MC sc in last 5 sts.

Row 10: Ch 2, turn; (sc in next sc, dc in next sc) twice, with Color B sc in next sc, (work Cluster in next sc, sc in next sc) twice, with MC (dc in next sc, sc in next sc) twice, hdc in last sc.

Row 11: Ch 1, turn; sc in first 5 sts, with Color B sc in next 4 sts, with MC sc in last 6 sts.

Row 12: Ch 2, turn; dc in next sc, (sc in next sc, dc in next sc) twice, with Color B sc in next sc, work Cluster in next sc, sc in next sc, with MC dc in next sc, (sc in next sc, dc in next sc) twice, hdc in last sc.

Row 13: Ch 1, turn; sc in first 6 sts, with Color B sc in next 2 sts, with MC sc in last 7 sts.

Row 14: Ch 2, turn; (sc in next sc, dc in next sc) 3 times; cut MC, with Color B sc in next sc; cut Color B, with MC (dc in next sc, sc in next sc) 3 times, hdc in last sc.

Row 15: Ch 1, turn; sc in each st across; do **not** finish off: 15 sc.

EDGING

Rnd 1: Ch 1, turn; (sc, ch 2, sc) in first sc, dc in next sc, (sc in next sc, dc in next sc) 6 times, (sc, ch 2, sc) in last sc (corner made); working in end of rows, dc in next row, (sc in next row, dc in next row) 6 times; working in free loops of beginning ch *(Fig. 19b, page 140)*, (sc, ch 2, sc) in first ch, dc in next ch, (sc in next ch, dc in next ch) 6 times, (sc, ch 2, sc) in last ch; working in end of rows, dc in next row, (sc in next row, dc in next row) 6 times; join with slip st to first sc, finish off.

Rnd 2: With **right** side facing, join Color A with sc in first sc to left of any corner ch-2 sp *(see Joining With Sc, page 140)*; (ch 2, skip next dc, sc in next sc) 7 times, ch 3, skip next ch-2 sp, ★ sc in next sc, (ch 2, skip next dc, sc in next sc) 7 times, ch 3, skip next ch-2 sp; repeat from ★ around; join with slip st to first sc, finish off.

Rnd 3: With **right** side facing, join MC with sc in first sc to **left** of any corner ch-3 sp; working **behind** Rnd 2 ch-2 sps, (dc in next dc on Rnd 1, sc in next sc on Rnd 2) 7 times, [dc, (ch 1, dc) twice] in next ch-2 sp on Rnd 1 (corner), ★ sc in next sc on Rnd 2, (dc in next dc on Rnd 1, sc in next sc on Rnd 2) 7 times, [dc, (ch 1, dc) twice] in next ch-2 sp on Rnd 1; repeat from ★ around; join with slip st to first sc, finish off.

Rnd 4: With **right** side facing, join Color A with sc in first sc to **left** of any corner; [dc in next ch-2 sp on Rnd 2 *(Fig. 20, page 140)*, sc in next sc on Rnd 3] 7 times, sc in next dc and in next ch, (sc, ch 1, sc) in next dc, sc in next ch and in next dc, ★ sc in next sc, (dc in next ch-2 sp on Rnd 2, sc in next sc on Rnd 3) 7 times, sc in next dc and in next ch, (sc, ch 1, sc) in next dc, sc in next ch and in next dc; repeat from ★ around; join with slip st to first sc, finish off.

JOINING

Afghan is assembled by whipstitching 9 Squares into 6 vertical strips and then by whipstitching strips together, using Color A and working through both loops *(Fig. 23a, page 141)*.

BORDER

Note: Work decrease as follows: YO, insert hook in corner ch-1 sp, YO and pull up a loop, YO and draw through 2 loops on hook, YO, insert hook in corner ch-1 sp of next Square, YO and pull up a loop, YO and draw through 2 loops on hook, YO and draw through all 3 loops on hook.

Rnd 1: With **right** side facing, join Color A with sc in first sc to **left** of any corner ch-1 sp; (dc in next st, sc in next st) 10 times, [decrease, sc in next st, (dc in next st, sc in next st) 10 times] across to next corner ch-1 sp, (dc, ch 2, dc) in corner ch-1 sp, ★ sc in next st, (dc in next st, sc in next st) 10 times, [decrease, sc in next st, (dc in next st, sc in next st) 10 times] across to next corner ch-1 sp, (dc, ch 2, dc) in corner ch-1 sp; repeat from ★ around; join with slip st to first sc.

Rnd 2: Slip st in next dc, ch 1, sc in same st, ch 1, ★ (skip next sc, sc in next st, ch 1) across to next corner ch-2 sp, (sc, ch 1) twice in corner ch-2 sp, sc in next st, ch 1; repeat from ★ around; join with slip st to first sc, finish off.

Rnd 3: With **right** side facing, join MC with slip st in any ch-1 sp; ch 1, (skip next sc, slip st in next ch-1 sp, ch 1) around to last sc, skip last sc; join with slip st to first st, finish off.

SIMPLE STRIPES

Simple stripes dress up this traditional throw, creating a versatile accent that will complement a variety of decors. Crocheted using a large hook and holding two strands of yarn together, it's quick and easy to make.

Finished Size: Approximately 46″ x 64″

MATERIALS
Worsted Weight Yarn, approximately:
  MC (Beige Heather) - 54 ounces,
    (1,540 grams, 3,395 yards)
  Color A (Green) - 4 ounces, (110 grams, 250 yards)
  Color B (Red) - 4 ounces, (110 grams, 250 yards)
Crochet hook, size P (12.00 mm) **or** size needed for gauge

GAUGE: In pattern, 10 sts and 6 rows = 4″

Note: Entire afghan is worked holding two strands of yarn together.

With MC, ch 159 **loosely**.

Row 1 (Right side): Sc in second ch from hook and in each ch across: 158 sc.

Note: Loop a short piece of yarn around any stitch to mark last row as **right** side.

Row 2: Ch 1, turn; sc in first 2 sc, (ch 2, skip next 2 sc, sc in next 2 sc) across: 39 ch-2 sps.

Row 3: Ch 3 **(counts as first dc, now and throughout)**, turn; 4 dc in each ch-2 sp across, skip next sc, dc in last sc: 158 dc.

Row 4: Ch 1, turn; sc in first 2 dc, (ch 2, skip next 2 dc, sc in next 2 dc) across.

Rows 5 and 6: Repeat Rows 3 and 4; at end of Row 6 finish off.

Row 7: With **right** side facing, join Color A with slip st in first sc; ch 3, 4 dc in each ch-2 sp across, skip next sc, dc in last sc.

Row 8: Ch 1, turn; sc in first 2 dc, (ch 2, skip next 2 dc, sc in next 2 dc) across; finish off.

Row 9: With **right** side facing, join MC with slip st in first sc; ch 3, 4 dc in each ch-2 sp across, skip next sc, dc in last sc.

Row 10: Ch 1, turn; sc in first 2 dc, (ch 2, skip next 2 dc, sc in next 2 dc) across; finish off.

Row 11: With **right** side facing, join Color B with slip st in first sc; ch 3, 4 dc in each ch-2 sp across, skip next sc, dc in last sc.

Row 12: Ch 1, turn; sc in first 2 dc, (ch 2, skip next 2 dc, sc in next 2 dc) across; finish off.

Row 13: Repeat Row 9.

Row 14: Repeat Row 4.

Rows 15-58: Repeat Rows 3 and 4, 22 times; at end of Row 58 finish off.

Rows 59 and 60: Repeat Rows 11 and 12.

Rows 61 and 62: Repeat Rows 9 and 10.

Rows 63-65: Repeat Rows 7-9.

Row 66: Repeat Row 4.

Rows 67 and 68: Repeat Rows 3 and 4.

Row 69: Ch 1, turn; sc in first 2 sc, (2 sc in next ch-2 sp, sc in next 2 sc) across; finish off.

Add fringe *(Figs. 25a & b, page 142)*.

BOLD WINTER WAVES

*Simple crochet stitches are used to create this extra-easy throw,
which features bold waves of color. Fashion it in our masculine color
scheme, or choose your own favorite wintertime colors.*

Finished Size: Approximately 47″ x 60″

MATERIALS
Worsted Weight Yarn, approximately:
  MC (Beige Heather) - 31 ounces,
    (880 grams, 1,950 yards)
  Color A (Green) - 8 ounces,
    (230 grams, 505 yards)
  Color B (Red) - 8 ounces, (230 grams, 505 yards)
  Color C (Blue) - 8 ounces, (230 grams, 505 yards)
  Crochet hook, size P (12.00 mm) **or** size needed for
  gauge

GAUGE: 9 sts = 4″ and 8 rows = 4¾″

Note: Entire afghan is worked holding two strands of
yarn together.

With MC, ch 104 **loosely**.
Row 1 (Right side): Dc in fourth ch from hook and in
next 4 chs, (sc in next 6 chs, dc in next 6 chs) across:
102 sts.
Note: Loop a short piece of yarn around any stitch to
mark last row as **right** side.
Row 2: Ch 3 **(counts as first dc, now and throughout)**,
turn; dc in next 5 dc, sc in next 6 sc, (dc in next 6 dc, sc
in next 6 sc) across to last 6 sts, dc in next 5 dc, dc in top
of beginning ch; finish off.
Row 3: With **right** side facing, join Color A with slip st
in first dc; ch 1, sc in same st and in next 5 dc, (dc in
next 6 sc, sc in next 6 dc) across.
Row 4: Ch 1, turn; sc in first 6 sc, (dc in next 6 dc, sc in
next 6 sc) across; finish off.
Row 5: With **right** side facing, join MC with slip st in
first sc; ch 3, dc in next 5 sc, (sc in next 6 dc, dc in next
6 sc) across.
Row 6: Ch 3, turn; dc in next 5 dc, (sc in next 6 sc, dc in
next 6 dc) across; finish off.
Row 7: With **right** side facing, join Color B with slip st
in first dc; ch 1, sc in same st and in next 5 dc, (dc in
next 6 sc, sc in next 6 dc) across.

Row 8: Ch 1, turn; sc in first 6 sc, (dc in next 6 dc, sc in
next 6 sc) across; finish off.
Row 9: With **right** side facing, join MC with slip st in
first sc; ch 3, dc in next 5 sc, (sc in next 6 dc, dc in next
6 sc) across.
Row 10: Ch 3, turn; dc in next 5 dc, (sc in next 6 sc,
dc in next 6 dc) across; finish off.
Row 11: With **right** side facing, join Color C with
slip st in first dc; ch 1, sc in same st and in next 5 dc,
(dc in next 6 sc, sc in next 6 dc) across.
Row 12: Ch 1, turn; sc in first 6 sc, (dc in next 6 dc, sc in
next 6 sc) across; finish off.
Row 13: With **right** side facing, join MC with slip st in
first sc; ch 3, dc in next 5 sc, (sc in next 6 dc, dc in next
6 sc) across.
Row 14: Ch 3, turn; dc in next 5 dc, (sc in next 6 sc,
dc in next 6 dc) across; finish off.
Rows 15-98: Repeat Rows 3-14, 7 times; at end of
Row 98, do **not** finish off.

EDGING

Rnd 1: Ch 1, turn; 3 sc in first dc, sc in next 5 dc, dc in
next 6 sc, (sc in next 6 dc, dc in next 6 sc) across to last
6 dc, sc in next 5 dc, 3 sc in last dc; working in end of
rows, sc evenly across; working in free loops of
beginning ch *(Fig. 19b, page 140)*, 3 sc in first ch, sc in
next 5 chs, dc in next 6 chs, (sc in next 6 chs, dc in next
6 chs) across to last 6 chs, sc in next 5 chs, 3 sc in last ch;
working in end of rows, sc evenly across; join with
slip st to first sc.
Rnd 2: Ch 1, sc in same st, 3 sc in next sc, sc in each st
around, working 3 sc in each corner sc; join with slip st
to first sc.
Rnd 3: Ch 1, working in Back Loops Only *(Fig. 18,
page 140)*, sc in same st and in next sc, 3 sc in next sc, sc
in each st around, working 3 sc in each corner sc; join
with slip st to first sc, finish off.

SNOWBALLS

Clear blue skies and a blanket of snow call for a trip outdoors. But when you return, you can cuddle up with this winter wonderland wrap. The puffy white clusters are reminiscent of fun-filled snowball fights.

Finished Size: Approximately 49" x 70"

MATERIALS
Worsted Weight Yarn, approximately:
MC (Blue) - 23 ounces, (650 grams, 1,515 yards)
CC (Ecru) - 29 ounces, (820 grams, 1,905 yards)
Crochet hooks, sizes G (4.00 mm) **and** I (5.50 mm)
or sizes needed for gauge

GAUGE: In pattern, with larger size hook,
20 sts and 19 rows = 4"

Note #1: Afghan is worked from side to side.
Note #2: Always join yarn and finish off leaving a 9"
end for Fringe.

CLUSTER
★ YO, insert hook in ch indicated, YO and pull up a loop, YO and draw through 2 loops on hook; repeat from ★ 2 times **more**, YO and draw through all 4 loops on hook *(Figs. 9a & b, page 135)*. Push Cluster to **right** side.

With larger size hook and MC, ch 348.
Row 1 (Right side)**:** Slip st in second ch from hook, (ch 1, skip next ch, slip st in next ch) across; finish off: 347 sts.
Note: Loop a short piece of yarn around any stitch to mark last row as **right** side.
Row 2: With **wrong** side facing and working in BLO *(Fig. 18, page 140)*, join CC with slip st in first slip st; (ch 1, skip next ch, slip st in next slip st) across; finish off.
Row 3: With **right** side facing and working in FLO, join MC with slip st in first slip st; (ch 1, skip next st, slip st in next slip st) across; finish off.
Row 4: With **wrong** side facing and working in BLO, join CC with slip st in first slip st; (ch 1, skip next ch, slip st in next slip st) twice, work Cluster in next ch, slip st in next slip st, ★ (ch 1, skip next ch, slip st in next slip st) 7 times, work Cluster in next ch, slip st in next slip st; repeat from ★ across to last 4 sts, (ch 1, skip next ch, slip st in next slip st) twice; finish off: 22 Clusters.
Row 5: With **right** side facing and working in FLO, join MC with slip st in first slip st; (ch 1, skip next st, slip st in next slip st) across; finish off.
Row 6: With **wrong** side facing and working in BLO, join CC with slip st in first slip st; ch 1, skip next ch, slip st in next slip st, work Cluster in next ch, slip st in next slip st, ch 1, skip next ch, slip st in next slip st, work Cluster in next ch, slip st in next slip st, ★ (ch 1, skip next ch, slip st in next slip st) 5 times, work Cluster in next ch, slip st in next slip st, ch 1, skip next ch, slip st in next slip st, work Cluster in next ch, slip st in next slip st; repeat from ★ across to last 2 sts, ch 1, skip next ch, slip st in last slip st; finish off: 44 Clusters.
Rows 7-9: Repeat Rows 3-5.
Rows 10-13: Repeat Rows 2 and 3, twice.
Row 14: With **wrong** side facing and working in BLO, join CC with slip st in first slip st; (ch 1, skip next ch, slip st in next slip st) 6 times, work Cluster in next ch, slip st in next slip st, ★ (ch 1, skip next ch, slip st in next slip st) 7 times, work Cluster in next ch, slip st in next slip st; repeat from ★ across to last 12 sts, (ch 1, skip next ch, slip st in next slip st) 6 times; finish off: 21 Clusters.
Row 15: With **right** side facing and working in FLO, join MC with slip st in first slip st; (ch 1, skip next st, slip st in next slip st) across; finish off.
Row 16: With **wrong** side facing and working in BLO,

join CC with slip st in first slip st; (ch 1, skip next ch, slip st in next slip st) 5 times, ★ work Cluster in next ch, slip st in next slip st, ch 1, skip next ch, slip st in next slip st, work Cluster in next ch, slip st in next slip st, (ch 1, skip next ch, slip st in next slip st) 5 times; repeat from ★ across; finish off: 42 Clusters.

Row 17: With **right** side facing and working in FLO, join MC with slip st in first slip st; (ch 1, skip next st, slip st in next slip st) across; finish off.

Rows 18 and 19: Repeat Rows 14 and 15.

Rows 20-23: Repeat Rows 2 and 3, twice.

Repeat Rows 4-23 for pattern until afghan measures approximately 49″, ending by working Row 11.

Change to smaller size hook.

Last Row - First Edging: With **right** side facing and working in both loops, join MC with slip st in first slip st; (ch 1, skip next ch, slip st in next slip st) across; finish off.

Second Edging: With **right** side facing and working in free loops of beginning ch *(Fig. 19b, page 140)*, join MC with slip st in first ch; (ch 1, skip next ch, slip st in next ch) across; finish off.

Add fringe *(Figs. 25a & b, page 142)*.

COUNTRY BLOCKS

Featuring blocks outlined with lacy openwork, this pretty afghan will coordinate beautifully with your patchwork quilts and other country accessories.

Finished Size: Approximately 49″ x 62″

MATERIALS
Worsted Weight Yarn, approximately:
58 ounces, (1,650 grams, 3,645 yards)
Crochet hook, size P (12.00 mm) **or** size needed for gauge

GAUGE: In pattern, 9 sts and 4 rows = 4″

Note: Entire afghan is worked holding two strands of yarn together.

Ch 110 **loosely**.

Row 1: Dc in sixth ch from hook, (ch 1, skip next ch, dc in next ch) across: 53 sps.

Row 2 (Right side): Ch 4 **(counts as first dc plus ch 1, now and throughout)**, turn; ★ dc in next dc, (dc in next ch-1 sp, dc in next dc) 3 times, ch 1; repeat from ★ across to last sp, skip next ch, dc in next ch: 93 dc.

Note: Work Puff St as follows: (YO, insert hook in stitch indicated, YO and pull up a loop even with hook) 4 times, YO and draw through all 9 loops on hook.

Row 3: Ch 4, turn; ★ dc in next 3 dc, work Puff St in next dc, dc in next 3 dc, ch 1; repeat from ★ across to last sp, dc in last dc: 13 Puff Sts.

Row 4: Ch 4, turn; ★ dc in next 3 dc, dc in next Puff St, dc in next 3 dc, ch 1; repeat from ★ across to last sp, dc in last dc.

Row 5: Ch 4, turn; dc in next dc, ★ (ch 1, skip next dc, dc in next dc) 3 times, ch 1, dc in next dc; repeat from ★ across.

Row 6: Ch 4, turn; dc in next dc, ★ (dc in next ch-1 sp, dc in next dc) 3 times, ch 1, dc in next dc; repeat from ★ across.

Rows 7-61: Repeat Rows 3-6, 13 times; then repeat Rows 3-5 once **more**; do **not** finish off.

EDGING

Ch 1, turn; (sc, ch 3) twice in first ch-1 sp, (sc in next sp, ch 3) across to next corner sp, ★ (sc, ch 3) 3 times in corner sp, (sc in next sp, ch 3) across to next corner sp; repeat from ★ 2 times **more**, sc in first corner sp, ch 3; join with slip st to first sc, finish off.

A CHILD'S VERY OWN

For a Christmas surprise, let Santa bring your favorite little one an afghan of his or her very own. This colorful throw is sure to brighten playtime and naptime alike.

Finished Size: Approximately 36″ x 36″

MATERIALS
 Worsted Weight Yarn, approximately:
  Color A (Red) - 2½ ounces, (70 grams, 165 yards)
  Color B (Yellow) - 3 ounces, (90 grams, 200 yards)
  Color C (Green) - 3½ ounces,
   (100 grams, 230 yards)
  Color D (Blue) - 4½ ounces,
   (130 grams, 295 yards)
  Color E (Purple) - 5 ounces,
   (140 grams, 330 yards)
 Crochet hook, size H (5.00 mm) **or** size needed for gauge

GAUGE: 14 dc and 9 rows = 4″

With Color A ch 4; join with slip st to form a ring.
Rnd 1 (Right side)**:** Ch 3 **(counts as first dc, now and throughout)**, 2 dc in ring, ch 1, (3 dc in ring, ch 1) 3 times; join with slip st to first dc: 12 dc.
Note: Loop a short piece of yarn around any stitch to mark last round as **right** side.

Rnd 2: Slip st in next dc, ch 3, turn; (3 dc, ch 1, 3 dc) in next ch-1 sp, ★ skip next dc, dc in next dc, (3 dc, ch 1, 3 dc) in next ch-1 sp; repeat from ★ around; join with slip st to first dc: 28 dc.
Rnd 3: Ch 3, turn; ★ dc in next dc and in each dc across to next corner ch-1 sp, 3 dc in ch-1 sp; repeat from ★ 3 times **more**, dc in each dc across; join with slip st to first dc: 40 dc.
Rnd 4: Ch 3, turn; ★ dc in next dc and in each dc across to next corner dc, (2 dc, ch 1, 2 dc) in corner dc; repeat from ★ 3 times **more**, dc in each dc across; join with slip st to first dc, finish off: 52 dc.
Note: Work Front Post treble crochet **(abbreviated FPtr)** as follows: YO twice, insert hook from **front** to **back** around post of dc one row **below** next dc, YO and pull up a loop *(Fig. 13d, page 138)*, (YO and draw through 2 loops on hook) 3 times, skip dc **behind** FPtr.
Rnd 5: With **right** side facing, join Color B with slip st in any corner ch-1 sp; ch 3, 2 dc in same sp, working in Back Loops Only *(Fig. 18, page 140)*, dc in next 6 dc, work FPtr, dc in next 6 dc, ★ 3 dc in next ch-1 sp, dc in next 6 dc, work FPtr, dc in next 6 dc; repeat from ★ 2 times **more**; join with slip st to first dc: 64 sts.
Rnd 6: Ch 3, turn; working in **both** loops, ★ dc in next dc and in each st across to next corner dc, (2 dc, ch 1, 2 dc) in corner dc; repeat from ★ around; join with slip st to first dc: 76 dc.
Rnd 7: Ch 3, turn; dc in next 2 dc, 3 dc in next ch-1 sp, ★ dc in each dc across to next corner ch-1 sp, 3 dc in ch-1 sp; repeat from ★ 2 times **more**, dc in each dc across; join with slip st to first dc: 88 dc.
Rnd 8: Ch 3, turn; ★ dc in next dc and each dc across to next corner dc, (2 dc, ch 1, 2 dc) in corner dc; repeat from ★ 3 times **more**, dc in last 3 dc; join with slip st to first dc, finish off: 100 dc.
Rnd 9: With **right** side facing, join Color C with slip st in any corner ch-1 sp; ch 3, 2 dc in same sp, ★ † working in Back Loops Only, dc in next 6 dc, work FPtr, dc in next 11 dc, work FPtr, dc in next 6 dc †, 3 dc in next ch-1 sp; repeat from ★ 2 times **more**, then repeat from † to † once; join with slip st to first dc: 112 sts.
Rnds 10-12: Repeat Rnds 6-8: 148 dc.
Rnd 13: With **right** side facing, join Color D with slip st in any corner ch-1 sp; ch 3, 2 dc in same sp,

★ † working in Back Loops Only, dc in next 6 dc, work FPtr, (dc in next 11 dc, work FPtr) across to within 6 dc of next corner ch-1 sp, dc in next 6 dc †, 3 dc in next ch-1 sp; repeat from ★ 2 times **more**, then repeat from † to † once; join with slip st to first dc: 160 sts.

Rnds 14-16: Repeat Rnds 6-8: 196 dc.
Rnds 17-40: Repeat Rnds 13-16 in the following stripe sequence: 4 rnds **each** of Color E, Color A, Color B, Color C, Color D, and Color E: 484 dc.
Finish off.

RICH HEATHER

Super-quick to make, this colorful mesh afghan is crocheted holding two strands of yarn together. We created the rich heathery effect by combining teal yarn with variegated lavender.

Finished Size: Approximately 47" x 68"

MATERIALS
 Worsted Weight Yarn, approximately:
  MC (Teal) - 29 ounces, (820 grams, 1,845 yards)
  CC (Variegated) - 22 ounces,
   (620 grams, 1,400 yards)
 Crochet hook, size Q (15.00 mm) **or** size needed for gauge

GAUGE: In pattern, (decrease, ch 1) 3 times
    and 5 rows = 4"

Note: Entire afghan is worked holding one strand of MC and one strand of CC together.

Ch 72 **loosely**.
Row 1 (Right side): Insert hook in second ch from hook and pull up a loop, insert hook in next ch and pull up a loop, YO and draw through all 3 loops on hook, ch 1, ★ (insert hook in next ch and pull up a loop) twice, YO and draw through all 3 loops on hook, ch 1; repeat from ★ across to last ch, sc in last ch: 71 sts.
Row 2: Ch 1, turn; [insert hook in same st and pull up a loop, insert hook in next ch-1 sp and pull up a loop, YO and draw through all 3 loops on hook (**beginning decrease made**)], ch 1, ★ [insert hook in next st and pull up a loop, insert hook in next ch-1 sp and pull up a loop, YO and draw through all 3 loops on hook (**decrease made**)], ch 1; repeat from ★ across to last st, sc in last st.
Repeat Row 2 until afghan measures approximately 68", ending by working a **right** side row.
Finish off.

Add fringe *(Figs. 25a & b, page 142)*.

WINTER WHITE

This luxurious throw is as soft and beautiful as a snowdrift.
Worked using two strands of yarn, it's surprisingly quick to make,
too. A lush tasseled fringe lends an air of elegance.

Finished Size: Approximately 48" x 63"

MATERIALS
   Worsted Weight Yarn, approximately:
   56 ounces, (1,590 grams, 3,840 yards)
   Crochet hook, size N (10.00 mm) **or** size needed for
   gauge

GAUGE: In pattern, 10 sts and 5 rows = 4"

Note: Entire Afghan is worked holding two strands of
yarn together.

Ch 122 **loosely.**
Row 1 (Right side): Sc in second ch from hook and in
next ch, skip next 3 chs, (3 dc, ch 1, 3 dc) in next ch
(Shell made), ★ skip next 3 chs, sc in next ch, ch 1, skip
next ch, sc in next ch, skip next 3 chs, work Shell in
next ch; repeat from ★ across to last 5 chs, skip next
3 chs, sc in last 2 chs: 12 Shells.
Note: Loop a short piece of yarn around any stitch to
mark last row as **right** side.
Row 2: Ch 2 **(counts as first hdc)**, turn; hdc in same sc,
ch 3, sc in next Shell (ch-1 sp), ch 3, ★ (hdc, ch 1, hdc) in

next ch-1 sp **(V-St made)**, ch 3, sc in next Shell, ch 3;
repeat from ★ across to last 2 sc, skip next sc, 2 hdc in
last sc.
Row 3: Ch 3 **(counts as first dc)**, turn; 3 dc in same
hdc, sc in next ch-3 sp, ch 1, sc in next ch-3 sp, ★ work
Shell in next V-St (ch-1 sp), sc in next ch-3 sp, ch 1, sc in
next ch-3 sp; repeat from ★ across to last 2 hdc, skip
next hdc, 4 dc in last hdc.
Row 4: Ch 1, turn; sc in first dc, ch 3, work V-St in
next ch-1 sp, ch 3, ★ sc in next Shell, ch 3, work V-St in
next ch-1 sp, ch 3; repeat from ★ across to last 4 dc, skip
next 3 dc, sc in last dc.
Row 5: Ch 1, turn; sc in first sc and in next ch-3 sp,
work Shell in next V-St, sc in next ch-3 sp, ★ ch 1, sc in
next ch-3 sp, work Shell in next V-St, sc in next ch-3 sp;
repeat from ★ across to last sc, sc in last sc.
Repeat Rows 2-5 for pattern until Afghan measures
approximately 62", ending by working Row 5.

EDGING

Ch 1, do **not** turn; sc evenly around, working 3 sc in
each corner; join with slip st to first sc, finish off.

Add fringe **(Figs. 25a & b, page 142)**.

YARN

Yarn listed under Materials for each afghan in this book is given as a generic weight. Once you know the **weight** of the yarn, **any** brand of the same **weight** may be used. This enables you to purchase the brand of yarn you like best.

You may wish to purchase a single skein first and crochet a gauge swatch. Compare the way your yarn looks to the photograph to be sure that you'll be satisfied with the results. How many skeins to buy depends on the yardage. Ounces and grams can vary from one brand of the same weight to another, but the yardage required will always remain the same.

ABBREVIATIONS

BLO	Back Loop(s) Only	MC	Main Color
CC	Contrasting Color	mm	millimeters
ch(s)	chain(s)	PC	Popcorn(s)
dc	double crochet(s)	Rnd(s)	Round(s)
dtr	double treble crochet(s)	sc	single crochet(s)
FLO	Front Loop(s) Only	sp(s)	space(s)
FPdc	Front Post double crochet(s)	st(s)	stitch(es)
FPhdc	Front Post half double crochet(s)	tr	treble crochet(s)
FPtr	Front Post treble crochet(s)	YO	yarn over
hdc	half double crochet(s)		

★ — work instructions following ★ as many **more** times as indicated in addition to the first time.

✝ to ✝ — work all instructions from first ✝ to second ✝ **as many** times as specified.

( ) or [ ] — work enclosed instructions **as many** times as specified by the number immediately following **or** work all enclosed instructions in the stitch or space indicated **or** contains explanatory remarks.

GAUGE

Correct gauge is essential for proper size. Hook size given in instructions is merely a guide and should never be used without first making a sample swatch approximately 4" square in the stitch, yarn, and hook specified. Then measure it, counting your stitches and rows carefully. If your swatch is smaller than specified, try again with a larger size hook; if larger, try again with a smaller size. Keep trying until you find the size that will give you the specified gauge. DO NOT HESITATE TO CHANGE HOOK SIZE TO OBTAIN CORRECT GAUGE.

BASIC STITCH GUIDE

CHAIN

When beginning a first row of crochet in a chain, always skip the first chain from the hook, and work into the second chain from hook (for single crochet) or third chain from hook (for half double crochet), etc. *(Fig. 1)*.

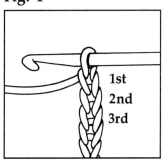

Fig. 1

1st
2nd
3rd

WORKING INTO THE CHAIN

Method 1: Insert hook into back ridge of each chain *(Fig. 2a)*.
Method 2: Insert hook under top two strands of each chain *(Fig. 2b)*.

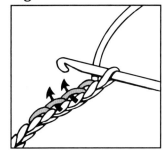

Fig. 2a

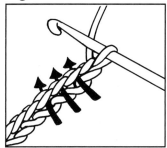

Fig. 2b

SINGLE CROCHET

Insert hook in stitch or space indicated, YO and pull up a loop, YO and draw through both loops on hook *(Fig. 3)* **(single crochet made, abbreviated sc)**.

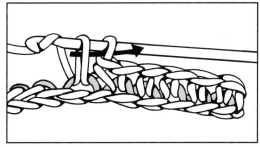

Fig. 3

LONG SINGLE CROCHET

Insert hook in stitch indicated, YO and pull up a loop even with loop on hook, YO and draw through both loops on hook *(Fig. 4)* **(Long single crochet made, abbreviated Long sc)**.

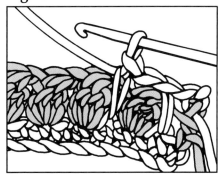

Fig. 4

HALF DOUBLE CROCHET

YO, insert hook in stitch or space indicated, YO and pull up a loop, YO and draw through all 3 loops on hook *(Fig. 5)* **(half double crochet made, abbreviated hdc)**.

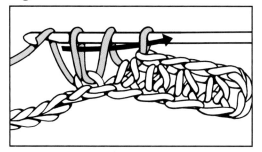

Fig. 5

DOUBLE CROCHET

YO, insert hook in stitch or space indicated, YO and pull up a loop, YO and draw through 2 loops on hook *(Fig. 6a)*, YO and draw through remaining 2 loops on hook *(Fig. 6b)* **(double crochet made, abbreviated dc)**.

Fig. 6a

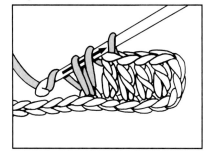

Fig. 6b

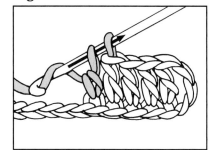

TREBLE CROCHET

YO twice, insert hook in stitch or space indicated, YO and pull up a loop *(Fig. 7a)*, (YO and draw through 2 loops on hook) 3 times *(Fig. 7b)* **(treble crochet made, abbreviated tr)**.

Fig. 7a

Fig. 7b

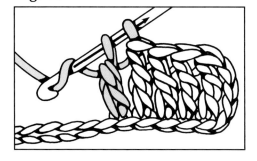

DOUBLE TREBLE CROCHET

YO three times, insert hook in stitch or space indicated, YO and pull up a loop, (YO and draw through 2 loops on hook) 4 times **(double treble crochet made, abbreviated dtr)**.

PATTERN STITCHES

CABLE

Ch 3 **loosely**, skip next 2 sc, sc in next sc *(Fig. 8a)*, **turn**, sc in each ch just completed *(Fig. 8b)*, slip st in next sc (sc before ch was begun) *(Fig. 8c)*, **turn**, working **behind** ch-3, sc in 2 skipped sc *(Fig. 8d,* **first Cable made)**, ★ ch 3 **loosely**, skip sc where previous ch was attached and next 2 sc, sc in next sc, **turn**, sc in each ch just completed, slip st in next sc (sc before ch was begun), **turn**, working **behind** ch-3, sc in 2 skipped sc **(Cable made)**.

Fig. 8a

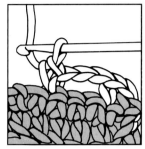

Fig. 8b

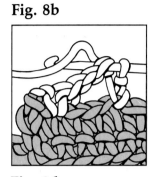

Fig. 8c

Fig. 8d

CLUSTER

A Cluster can be worked all in the same stitch or space *(Figs. 9a & b)*, **or** across several stitches *(Figs. 9c & d)*.

Fig. 9a

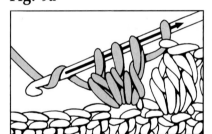

Fig. 9b

Fig. 9c

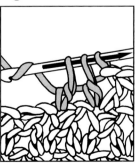

Fig. 9d

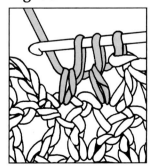

CROSS STITCH

Skip next stitch, dc in next stitch, working **around** dc just made, dc in skipped stitch *(Fig. 10)*.

Fig. 10

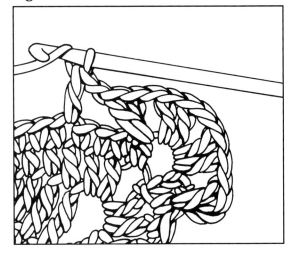

LEAVES

Working **below** next dc, insert hook in sc one row **below** and two sts to the **right**, YO and pull up a loop *(Fig. 11a)*, insert hook in dc two rows **below** and one st to the **right**, YO and pull up a loop, insert hook in sc three rows **below**, YO and pull up a loop, insert hook in dc two rows **below** and one st to the **left**, YO and pull up a loop, insert hook in sc one row **below** and two sts to the **left**, YO and pull up a loop, YO and draw through all 6 loops on hook *(Fig. 11b)*.

Fig. 11a

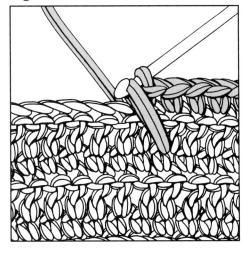

Fig. 11b

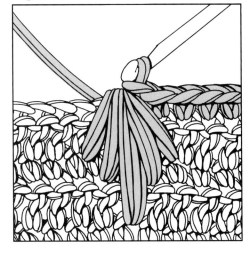

POPCORN

5 Dc in next stitch, drop loop from hook, insert hook in first dc of 5-dc group, hook dropped loop and draw through *(Fig. 12)*, ch 1 to close.

Fig. 12

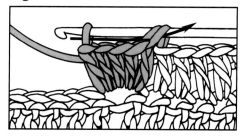

POST STITCH

Work around post of stitch indicated, inserting hook in direction of arrow *(Fig. 13a)*.

Fig. 13a

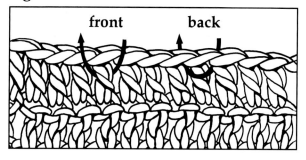

FRONT POST HDC

YO, insert hook from **front** to **back** around post of stitch indicated, YO and pull up a loop, YO and draw through all 3 loops on hook *(Fig. 13b)* **(Front post hdc made, abbreviated FPhdc)**.

Fig. 13b

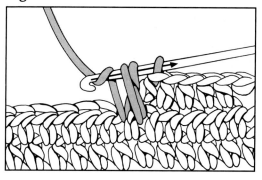

FRONT POST DC

YO, insert hook from **front** to **back** around post of stitch indicated, YO and pull up a loop *(Fig. 13c)*, (YO and draw through 2 loops on hook) twice **(Front Post dc made, abbreviated FPdc)**.

Fig. 13c

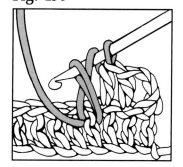

FRONT POST TR

YO twice, insert hook from **front** to **back** around post of stitch indicated, YO and pull up a loop *(Fig. 13d)*, (YO and draw through 2 loops on hook) 3 times, **(Front Post tr made, abbreviated FPtr)**.

Fig. 13d

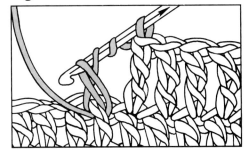

ENGLISH GARDEN

Working in **front** of first 2 dc on next row, work FPtr around post of third dc *(Fig. 14)*.

Fig. 14

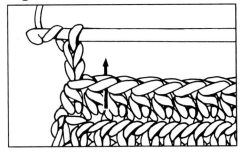

REVERSE HALF DOUBLE CROCHET

Working from **left** to **right**, YO, insert hook in stitch indicated *(Fig. 15a)*, YO and draw through, under and to left of loops on hook (3 loops on hook) *(Fig. 15b)*, YO and draw through all 3 loops on hook *(Fig. 15c)* **(reverse hdc made, *Fig. 15d*)**.

Fig. 15a

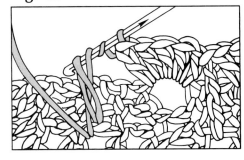

Fig. 15b

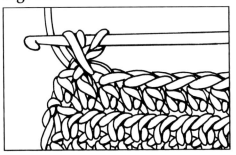

Fig. 15c

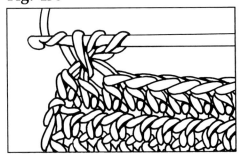

Fig. 15d

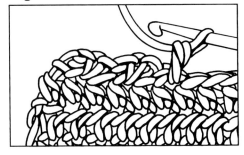

QUILT-BLOCKS

Join second Block to first Block with slip st around beginning ch of previous Block *(Fig. 16a)*, ch 3, 3 dc in same sp *(Fig. 16b)*.

Fig. 16a

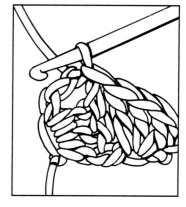

Fig. 16b

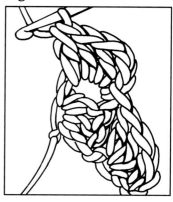

Symbol crochet chart illustrates Rows 1-7 of Quilt-Block Flowers Squares.

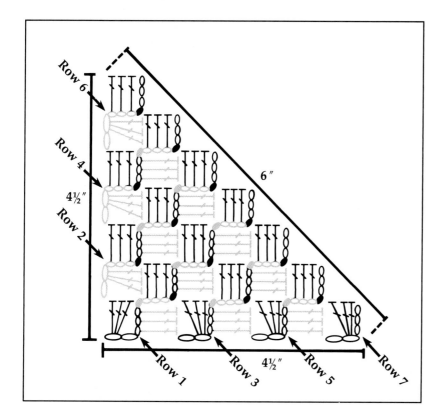

SYMBOL CROCHET KEY

○   chain

●   slip st

†   double crochet

STITCHING TIPS

BEGINNING LOOP

Leaving a 3″ end, wind yarn around finger once to form a ring, YO and draw through ring *(Fig. 17)*.

Fig. 17

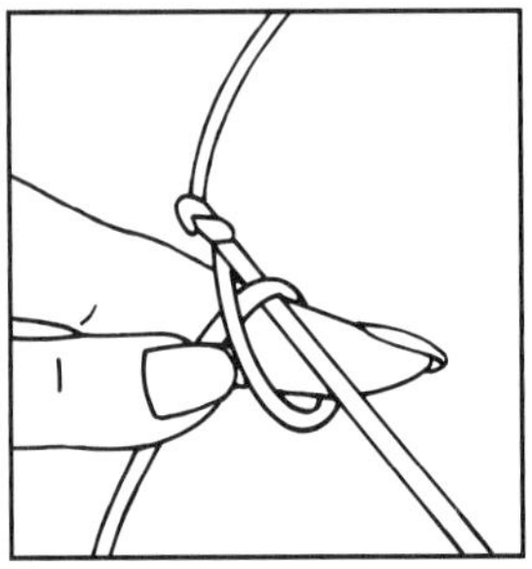

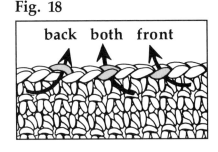

JOINING WITH SC

When instructed to join with sc, begin with a slip knot on hook. Insert hook in stitch or space indicated, YO and pull up a loop, yarn over and draw through both loops on hook.

BACK OR FRONT LOOP ONLY

Work only in loop(s) indicated by arrow *(Fig. 18)*.

Fig. 18

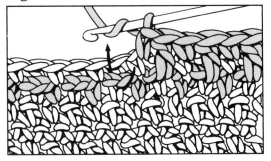

back   both   front

FREE LOOP

After working in Back or Front Loops Only on a row or round, there will be a ridge of unused loops. These are called the free loops. Later, when instructed to work in the free loops of the same row or round, work in these loops *(Fig. 19a)*. When instructed to work in a free loop of a beginning chain, work in loop indicated by arrow *(Fig. 19b)*.

Fig. 19a

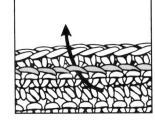

Fig. 19b

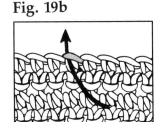

WORKING IN ROUND BELOW

When instructed to work in ch-2 sp one round **below** next dc, work in space indicated by arrow *(Fig. 20)*.

Fig. 20

CHANGING COLORS

Work the last stitch to within one step of completion, hook new yarn *(Fig. 21)* and draw through loops on hook. Cut old yarn and work over both ends unless otherwise specified.

Fig. 21

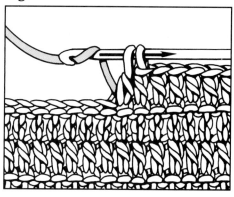

FINISHING

NO SEW JOINING

Hold Squares or Motifs with wrong sides together. Slip st into space indicated *(Fig. 22)*.

Fig. 22

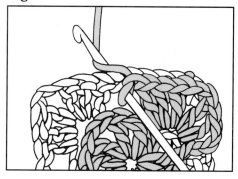

WHIPSTITCH

With **wrong** sides together, and beginning in corner stitch, sew through both pieces once to secure the beginning of the seam, leaving an ample yarn end to weave in later. Insert needle from **right** to **left** through both loops of **each** piece *(Fig. 23a)* **or** through inside loops *(Fig. 23b)*. Bring needle around and insert it from **right** to **left** through the next loops of **both** pieces. Continue in this manner, keeping the sewing yarn fairly loose.

Fig. 23a   **both loops**

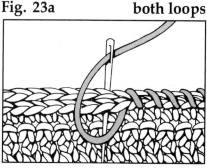

Fig. 23b   **inside loops**

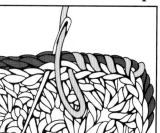

TASSEL

Cut a piece of cardboard 3″ wide and as long as you want your finished tassel to be. Wind a double strand of yarn around the cardboard approximately 20 times. Cut an 18″ length of yarn and insert it under all of the strands at the top of the cardboard; pull up **tightly** and tie securely. Leave the yarn ends long enough to attach the tassel. Cut the yarn at the opposite end of the cardboard **(Fig. 24a)** and then remove it. Cut a 6″ length of yarn and wrap it **tightly** around the tassel twice, ½″ below the top **(Fig. 24b)**; tie securely. Trim the ends.

Fig. 24a

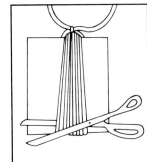

Fig. 24b

FRINGE

Cut a piece of cardboard 3″ wide and ½″ longer than you want your finished fringe to be. Wind the yarn **loosely** and **evenly** around the cardboard until the card is filled, then cut across one end; repeat as needed. Hold together half as many strands of yarn as needed for the finished fringe; fold in half.

With **wrong** side facing and using a crochet hook, draw the folded end up through a row or stitch and pull the loose ends through the folded end **(Fig. 25a)**; draw the knot up **tightly** **(Fig. 25b)**. Repeat, spacing as desired. Lay flat on a hard surface and trim the ends.

Fig. 25a

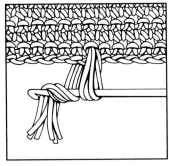

Fig. 25b

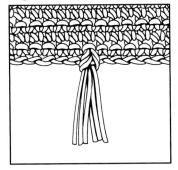

KNOTS

Working across one end, tie a knot with the first 3 strands (2 strands from the first row and one strand from the second row).
Tie a knot with the next 2 strands (one strand from the second row and one strand from the third row) **(Fig. 26)**. Continue in this manner until each strand has been used, tying last knot with the last 3 strands.

Fig. 26

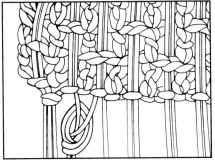

CREDITS

To Magna IV Color Imaging of Little Rock, Arkansas, we say thank you for the superb color reproduction and excellent pre-press preparation.

We want to especially thank photographers Ken West, Larry Pennington, Mark Mathews, and Karen Busick Shirey of Peerless Photography, Little Rock, Arkansas, and Jerry R. Davis of Jerry Davis Photography, Little Rock, Arkansas, for their time, patience, and excellent work.

We would like to extend a special word of thanks to the talented designers who created the lovely projects in this book.

Mary Lamb Becker: *Just for ''Ewe,''* page 38
Judy Bolin: *Baby-Soft Granny,* page 23, and *Rainbow Diamonds,* page 58
Anita Cordell: *Bubbles for Baby,* page 48
Eldonna Ewers: *Heritage Afghan,* page 60
Marion Graham: *Spring Ripple,* page 8
Nancy Griffin: *Candy Stripes,* page 108
Cathy Grivnow: *Quilt-Block Flowers,* page 43
Anne Halliday: *Diamond Classic,* page 12; *Perfect for the Porch,* page 40; *Irresistible Ripples,* page 52; *Elegant Daisy Chain,* page 56; *Textured Bands,* page 72; *Warm Autumn Wrap,* page 76; *Fireside Cheer,* page 106; *Christmas Trees,* page 115; and *Snowballs,* page 122
Cathy Hardy: *Precious in Pink,* page 18; *Pretty Panels,* page 86; and *A Child's Very Own,* page 126
Kathleen Harper: *Spring Clover,* page 14
Jan Hatfield: *Picket Fences,* page 50, and *English Garden,* page 102
Jean Holzman: *Stitch Sampler,* page 90
Irene Johnson: *Soft Stripes,* page 68
Lucia Karge: *A Dash of Red,* page 100
Terry Kimbrough: *Victorian Throw,* page 10; *Pretty Pansies,* page 16; *Rambling Roses,* page 20; *A Patchwork of Petals,* page 26; *Wildflower Wrap,* page 28; *Soft and Feminine,* page 34; *Delightful Daisies,* page 54; *Evergreens in Autumn,* page 84; *Rustic Ripple,* page 88; *Tantalizingly Teal,* page 104; *Simple Stripes,* page 118; *Bold Winter Waves,* page 120; *Country Blocks,* page 124; and *Rich Heather,* page 128
Linda Luder: *Winter White,* page 130
Jo Ann Maxwell: *Summer Favorite,* page 63
Penny McCusker: *Valentine Afghan,* page 111
Kay Fisher Meadors: *Autumn Leaves,* page 82
Marion Miedema: *Autumn Spice,* page 96
Diana Nelson: *Stained Glass Beauty,* page 74
Mary Jane Protus: *Flower Patch Afghan,* page 6
Rhonda Semonis: *Harvest Gold,* page 70
Mary Ann Sipes: *Fall Splendor,* page 78
Rena Stevens: *Timeless Blue and White,* page 30
Carole Rutter Tippett: *Fourth of July Fanfare,* page 46